How to Stubbornly Refuse to Make Yourself Miserable About Anything— Yes, Anything!

Books and Monographs by Albert Ellis

An Introduction to the Principles of Scientific Psychoanalysis

The Folklore of Sex

New Approaches to Psychotherapy Techniques

Sex, Society and the Individual (with A. P. Pillay)

Sex Life of the American Woman and the Kinsey Report

The American Sexual Tragedy

The Psychology of Sex Offenders (with Ralph Brancale)

How to Live with a "Neurotic"

Sex Without Guilt

What is Psychotherapy?

The Place of Value in the Practice of Psychotherapy

The Art and Science of Love

A Guide to Rational Living (with Robert A. Harper)

Creative Marriage (paperback edition title: A Guide to Successful
    Marriage) (with Robert A. Harper)

The Encyclopedia of Sexual Behavior (with Albert Abarbanel)

Reason and Emotion in Psychotherapy

If This Be Sexual Heresy . . .

The Origins and Development of the Incest Taboo

Sex and the Single Man

The Intelligent Woman's Guide to Manhunting

Nymphomania: A Study of the Over-sexed Woman (with Edward
    Sagarin)

Homosexuality

The Case for Sexual Liberty

Suppressed: Seven Key Essays Publishers Dared Not Print

The Search for Sexual Enjoyment

The Art of Erotic Seduction (with Roger O. Conway)

Is Objectivism a Religion?

How to Prevent Your Child from Becoming a Neurotic Adult
(paperback edition title: How to Raise an Emotionally Healthy,
Happy Child (with Janet L. Wolfe and Sandra Moseley)

Growth Through Reason (with Ben N. Ard, Jr., John M. Gullo, Paul A.
Hauck, Maxie C. Maultsby, Jr., and H. Jon Geis)

Executive Leadership: A Rational Approach

Sex and Sex Education: A Bibliography (with Flora C. Seruya and
Susan Losher)

Murder and Assassination (with John M. Gullo)

How to Master Your Fear of Flying

The Civilized Couple's Guide to Extramarital Adventure

The Sensuous Person: Critique and Corrections

Humanistic Psychotherapy: The Rational-Emotive Approach

A New Guide to Rational Living (with Robert A. Harper)

Sex and the Liberated Man

Anger: How to Live With and Without It

Overcoming Procrastination (with William Knaus)

Handbook of Rational-Emotive Therapy (with Russell Grieger)

A Garland of Rational Songs

The Intelligent Woman's Guide to Dating and Mating

Theoretical and Empirical Foundations of Rational-Emotive Therapy
(with John M. Whiteley)

A Guide to Personal Happiness (with Irving Becker)

Rational-Emotive Approaches to the Problems of Childhood
(with Michael E. Bernard)

Overcoming Resistance

Applications of Rational-Emotive Therapy to Problems of Living
(with Michael E. Bernard)

Rational-Emotive Therapy and Cognitive Behavior Therapy

How to Stubbornly Refuse to Make Yourself Miserable About Anything— Yes, Anything!

by Albert Ellis, Ph.D.

A LYLE STUART BOOK
Published by Carol Publishing Group

Carol Publishing Group Edition, 1996

A Lyle Stuart Book
Published by Carol Publishing Group
Lyle Stuart is a registered trademark of Carol Communications, Inc.

Editorial, sales and distribution, rights and permissions inquiries should be addressed to Carol Publishing Group, 120 Enterprise Avenue, Secaucus, N.J. 07094

In Canada: Canadian Manda Group, One Atlantic Avenue, Suite 105, Toronto, Ontario M6K 3E7

Carol Publishing Group books may be purchased in bulk at special discounts for sales promotions, fund-raising, or educational purposes. Special editions can be created to specifications. For details, contact Special Sales Department, 120 Enterprise Avenue, Secaucus, N.J. 07094

Manufactured in the United States of America
ISBN 0-8184-0456-6

20 19 18 17 16 15 14 13 12

Library of Congress Cataloging-in-Publication Data

Ellis, Albert.
    How to stubbornly refuse to make yourself miserable
about anything—yes, anything! / by Albert Ellis.
        p.   cm.
Bibliography : p.
Includes index.
1. Rational-emotive psychotherapy. I. Title.
RC489.R3E443   1988
616.89'14—dc19   87-37577
                                          CIP

Contents

How to Stubbornly Refuse to Make Yourself Miserable About Anything— Yes, Anything!

CHAPTER 1

Why Is This Book Different from Other Self-help Books?

Hundreds of self-help books are published every year, and many of them are truly helpful to millions of readers. Why bother to write another? Why should I try to surpass my own and Robert A. Harper's *A New Guide to Rational Living*, which has already sold over a million copies, and try to supplement derivative books, such as *Your Erroneous Zones*, which have also had literally millions of readers? Why bother?

For several important reasons. Although Rational-Emotive Therapy (RET), which I originated in 1955, is now a major part of the psychological scene today, and although most modern therapists (yes, even psychoanalysts) include big chunks of it in their treatment plans, it is often used in a watered-down, wishy-washy way.

Aside from my professional writing, no book as yet gives a hardheaded, straight-from-the-horse's-mouth version of RET; and those few that have attempted to do so are not written in simple, popular, self-help form.[1] The present volume aims to make up for this omission.

More specifically, this book has the following goals—which I do not think you will find presented, all together, in any other book on acquiring mental health and happiness.

- It encourages you to have and to express strong feelings when something goes wrong with your life. But it clearly distinguishes between your feeling appropriately and helpfully concerned, sorry, sad, frustrated, or annoyed and your feeling inappropriately and destructively panicked, depressed, enraged, and self-pitying.

• It shows you how to cope with difficult life situations and how to feel better when you are faced with them. But, more important—much more important—it demonstrates how you can *get better* as well as *feel better* when you needlessly "neuroticize" and plague yourself.

• It not only teaches you how you *can* control your emotional destiny and *can* stubbornly refuse to make yourself miserable over anything (yes, anything!), but it also specifically explains what you can *do* to use your potential for self-control.

• It rigorously stays with and promotes scientific thinking, reason, and reality, and it strictly avoids what most self-help books carelessly counsel today—huge amounts of mysticism, religiosity, and utopianism.

• It will help you achieve a profound philosophic change and a radically new outlook on life instead of a Pollyannaish "positive thinking" attitude that will only help you cope temporarily with difficulties and will often defeat you in the long run.

• It gives you many techniques for changing your personality, which are not backed merely by anecdotal or case-history "evidence," but which have now been proved to be effective by scores of objective, scientific experiments that were conducted with control groups.

• It efficiently shows you how you are *now* still creating your *present* emotional and behavioral problems, and it doesn't encourage you to waste endless time and energy foolishly trying to understand and explain your past history. It demonstrates how you *still* needlessly upset yourself and what you can do *today* to refuse to keep doing so.

• It encourages you to take full responsibility for your "upsetness" and for reducing it rather than copping out by blaming your parents or social conditions for your going along with their silly teachings.

• This book presents the ABCs of RET (and of other forms of cognitive and cognitive-behavioral therapy) in a simple, understandable way, and it shows how stimuli or Activating Events (A) in your life do not mainly or directly cause your emotional consequences (C). Instead, your Belief System (B) largely upsets you, and you therefore have the ability to

Dispute (D) these irrational Beliefs (iBs) and to change them. It especially shows you many thinking, many emotive, and many behavioral methods of disputing and surrendering your irrational Beliefs (iBs) and thereby arriving at an Effective New Philosophy (E) of life.

- It shows you not only how to keep your present desires, wishes, preferences, goals, and values; but how to give up your grandiose, godlike demands and commands—those absolutistic and dogmatic shoulds, oughts, and musts that you add to desires and preferences and by which you needlessly disturb yourself.

- It informs you how to be independent and inner-directed and how to think for *yourself* rather than be gullible and suggestible, going along with what *others* think you should think.

- It gives you many practical, action-oriented exercises, which you can use to *work at* and *practice* RET ways of rethinking and redoing your way of living.

- It shows you how to be rational in a highly irrational world— how to be as happy as *you* can be under some of the most difficult and "impossible" conditions. It insists that you can stubbornly refuse to make yourself miserable about some truly gruesome happenings—poverty, terrorism, sickness, war; and that you can, if you choose to do so, work more effectively to change some of the worst situations that confront you, and perhaps even the entire world.

- It will help you understand some of the main roots of mental disturbance—such as bigotry, intolerance, dogmatism, tyranny, and despotism—and to see how you can combat these roots of neurosis in yourself and in others.

- It presents a large variety of RET methods for dealing with severe feelings of anxiety, depression, hostility, self-denigration, and self-pity. More than any other major school of therapy, RET is truly eclectic and multimodal. At the same time, it is selective and does its best to eliminate harmful and inefficient methods of psychotherapy.

- RET is highly active-directive. It gets to the heart of human disturbance quickly and effectively, and presents self-help procedures that can be unusually effective in a short period of time.

- This book shows you how to be an honest hedonist and

individualist—to be true to thine own self first, but at the same time live happily, successfully, and relatedly in a social group. It lets you keep and even sharpen your own special values, goals, and ideals while being a responsible citizen of your chosen community.

• It is simple and, I hope, exceptionally clear, but far from simplistic. Its wisdom, gleaned from many philosophers and psychologists, is practical and earthy—but nonetheless profound.

• It presents rules and methods derived from today's fastest-growing type of therapies—RET (Rational-Emotive Therapy) and CBT (Cognitive-Behavioral Therapy)—which have grown enormously in recent years through their efficacy in helping millions of clients as well as thousands of therapists. It takes the best of the self-help techniques from which these therapies are formed and adapts them to the ability of the average reader to use them. That means Y-O-U.

Does this book, finally, uniquely tell you how to stubbornly refuse to make yourself miserable about anything—yes, anything? Really? Honestly? No nonsense about it? Yes, it actually does—if you will sincerely listen (L-I-S-T-E-N) and work (W-O-R-K) at receiving and using its message.

Will you listen?
Will you work?
Will you T-H-I-N-K?
You definitely can.
I hope you will!

CHAPTER 2

Can You Really Refuse to Make Yourself Miserable About Anything?

This book has a strange message, that practically all human misery and serious emotional turmoil are quite unnecessary—not to mention unethical. You, unethical? When you make yourself severely anxious or depressed, you clearly are acting against *you* and are being unfair and unjust to *yourself*.

Your disturbance also badly affects your social group. It helps to upset your relatives and friends and, to some extent, your whole community. The expense of making yourself panicked, enraged, and self-pitying is enormous. In time and money lost. In needless effort spent. In uncalled-for mental anguish. In sabotaging others' happiness. In foolishly frittering away potential joy during the one life—yes, the *one* life—you'll ever have.

What a waste. How unnecessary!

But isn't emotional pain the human condition? Yes, it is. Hasn't it been with us since time immemorial? Yes, it has. Isn't it, then, inevitable as long as we are truly human, as long as we have the capacity to feel?

No, it isn't.

Let us not confuse painful feelings with emotional disturbance. Humans distinctly *feel*. Other animals feel, too, but not as delicately. Dogs, for example, seem to feel what we may call love, sadness, fear, and pleasure. Not exactly as we do, but they definitely have feelings.

But how about awe? Romantic love? Poetic ardor? Creative passion? Scientific curiosity? Do dogs and chimpanzees have these feelings too?

I doubt it. Our subtle, romantic, creative feelings arise from complex thoughts and philosophies. As Epictetus and Marcus Aurelius, ancient stoic philosophers, pointed out, we humans mainly feel the way we think. No, not completely. But *mainly*.

That is the crucial message that Rational-Emotive Therapy (RET) has been making for over thirty years, after I adapted some of its principles from the ancients and from later thinkers— especially from Baruch Spinoza, Immanuel Kant, John Dewey, and Bertrand Russell. We *do* largely create our own feelings; and we do so by learning (from our parents and others) and by inventing (in our own heads) our own sane and foolish thoughts.

Create? Yes, *create*. We consciously and unconsciously *choose* to think and hence to feel in certain self-helping and self-harming ways.[1]

Not totally. Not altogether. Not by a long shot! For we have great help, if you want to call it that, from both our heredity and our environment.

No, we are hardly born with specific thoughts, feelings, and behaviors. Nor does our environment directly *make us* act or feel. But our genes and our social upbringing give us strong tendencies to do (and enjoy) what we do. And although we usually go along with (or indulge in) these tendencies, we don't exactly *have* to. We definitely don't.

Not that we have unlimited choice or free will. Heck, no. We can't, no matter how hard we try, flap our hands and fly. We can't easily stop our various addictions to substances such as cigarettes, food, and alcohol, or to habits such as procrastination. We have one hell of a time changing any of our fixed habits. Alas, we do!

But we *can* choose to change ourselves remarkably. We *are* able to alter our strongest thoughts, feelings, and actions. Why? Because unlike dogs, monkeys, and cockroaches, we are human. As humans, we are born with (and can escalate) a trait that other creatures rarely possess: the ability to think about our thinking. We are not only natural philosophers, we can philosophize about our philosophy, reason about our reasoning.

Which is damned lucky! And which gives us *some* degree of self-determination or free will. For if we were *just* one-level thinkers and could not *examine* our thinking, could not *weigh* our feelings, could not *review* our actions, where would we be? Pretty well stuck!

Actually, we are not stuck or habit-bound—if we *choose* not to be. For we can be aware of our surroundings and also aware of *ourselves*. We are born—yes, born—with a rare potential for observing and thinking about our *own* behavior. Not that other animals (primates, for example) have *no* self-consciousness. They do have *some*. But not very much.

We humans have real self-awareness. We *can*, though we do not *have to*, observe and judge our own goals, desires, and purposes. We *can* examine, review, and change them. We can also see and reflect upon our *changed* ideas, emotions, and doings. And we can change *them*. And change them again—and again![2]

Now let's not run this idea of "self-change" into the ground. Of course we *have* this capacity. Of course we *can* use it, but not without limits—not perfectly. We get our original goals and desires largely from our biological tendencies and from our early childhood training.

We *like* mother's milk (or bottled formulas), and we *enjoy* nestling up to our parents' bodies. We like mother's milk and parental cuddling because we are *born* to like them, are *trained* to like them, and become *habituated* to liking them. So what we call our desires and preferences are not all *freely* chosen. Many are instilled in us by our heredity and our conditioning.

The more we choose to *use* our self-awareness and to *think* about our goals and desires, the more we create—yes, create—free will or self-determination. That also goes for our emotions, both our healthy and our disturbed feelings. Take, for instance, your own feelings of frustration and disappointment when you suffer a loss. Someone promises to give you a job, for example, or lend you some money, and then backs down. Naturally, you feel annoyed and sad. Good. These negative feelings acknowledge that you are not getting what you want and encourage you to look for another job or another loan.

So, your feelings of annoyance and sadness are at first uncomfortable and "bad." In the long run, however, they tend to help you get more of what you want and less of what you don't want.

Do you have a choice of these healthy negative feelings when something goes wrong in your life? Yes. You may choose to feel *very* annoyed—or a little annoyed. You may choose to focus on the advantages of losing a promised job (such as the opportunity to try for a better one) and hardly feel annoyed at all. Or you may choose to put down the person who falsely promised you the job and feel happy about being a "better person" than this "louse."

You may also choose to highlight the disadvantages of getting the promised job (for example, the hassle of commuting to work) and actually make yourself feel quite pleased about not getting it. You might have to work at not feeling sad and annoyed about losing the job, but you could definitely *choose* to do so.

So you do have a choice about your *natural* or *normal* reactions to losing a job (or a loan or anything else). Usually, you would not bother to exert this choice, and you would choose to accept the normal, healthy feelings of annoyance and disappointment, using them in the future to help you. You would live with them and benefit from them.

Now let us suppose that when you are unfairly deprived of a job or a loan you make yourself feel severely anxious, depressed, self-denigrated, or enraged. You see that you are being treated unfairly. You upset yourself immensely about their unfairness.

Can you still choose to have or not have *these* very strong, off-the-wall feelings?

Definitely, yes. Clearly, you can.

That is the main theme of this book: No matter how badly you act, no matter how unfairly others treat you, no matter how crummy the conditions you live under are—you virtually always (*yes*, A-L-W-A-Y-S) have the ability and the power to change your intense feelings of anxiety, despair, and hostility. Not only can you decrease them, you can annihilate and remove them. *If* you use the methods outlined in the following chapters. If you *work* at using them!

When you suffer a real loss, are your feelings of panic, depression, and rage unnatural? No, they are so natural, so normal that they are a basic part of the human condition. They are exceptionally common and universal. Virtually all of us have them—and often! It would be most strange if you did not feel them fairly frequently.

But *normal* or *common* doesn't mean *healthy*. Colds are very common. So are bruises, broken bones, and infections. But they are hardly good or beneficial!

So it is with feelings of anxiety. Concern, caution, vigilance, and what we may call light anxiety are normal and *healthy*. If you had absolutely zero anxiety you would fail to watch where you're going or how you're doing, and you would soon get into trouble and perhaps even kill yourself.

But severe anxiety, nervousness, dread, and panic are normal (or frequent) but *un*healthy. Severity of anxiety leads to dismal *over*concern, to terror, and to horror. It can freeze you and help you to behave incompetently and unsocially. So by all means, keep your feelings of concern and caution but junk your feelings of overconcern, "awfulizing," panic, and dread.

How?

First, acknowledge that the two feelings are quite different and don't quibble or rationalize that anxiety is a healthy condition. Don't claim that anxiety is inevitable and has to be accepted as long as you live. No. Concern or caution is almost inevitable (and good) for you. But not panic and horror.

What is the difference between concern and panic?

The difference stems from seeing the things you desire as *absolute necessities*. As I pointed out in *A New Guide to Rational Living*, you create severe anxiety when you jump from inclination to "*must*urbation."

If you *prefer* to perform well and *want* to be accepted by others, you are *concerned* that you will fail and be rejected. Your healthy concern encourages you to act competently and nicely. But if you devoutly believe that you absolutely, under all conditions, *must* perform well and that you *have* to be accepted by others, you will then tend to make yourself—yes, *make* yourself—panicked if you don't perform as well as you supposedly *must*.[3]

What luck! If the theories of Epictetus, Karen Horney (who first talked about the "tyranny of the shoulds"), Alfred Korzybski (the founder of general semantics), and RET are correct, you almost always bring on your emotional problems by rigidly adopting one basic method of crooked thinking—*must*urbation. Therefore, if you understand how you upset yourself by slipping into irrational shoulds, oughts, demands, and commands, unconsciously sneaking them into your thinking, you can just about always stop disturbing yourself about anything.

Always? No, *just about* always.

For there are, as we shall discuss later, a few exceptions to the rule of *must*urbation. But in about ninety-five out of a hundred cases, you can spot your *must*urbatory thinking, quickly change it, and refuse to be miserable about the hassles that you "normally" upset yourself about.

Really?

Yes, really, as you can rationally figure out if you *think* about it.

Can I prove this RET claim? I think that I can. Modern psychology has done many experiments showing that panicked and depressed people have been able, by changing their outlook, to overcome their disturbed feelings and to lead much happier lives. Recently, thanks to researchers who do studies of Rational-Emotive Therapy, Cognitive Therapy, and other cognitive-behavioral therapies, we now have more than two hundred controlled scientific studies showing that teaching people how to change some of their negative ideas helps them to feel and act much better.[4] We also have hundreds of other studies indicating that the main techniques used in RET work effectively.

Still another batch of scientific studies—at the present writing, over 250 of them—have tested whether the main irrational Beliefs (iBs) that people hold (and that I pointed out in 1956) actually show how emotionally disturbed they are. About 95 percent of these studies show that people who have serious emotional problems admit that they have more irrational beliefs than people who have lesser problems.[5]

Does all this scientific evidence prove that you can easily discover your unconditional, rigid shoulds, oughts, musts, commands, and demands that make you miserable and soon give them up? Can you quickly become a clear thinker and thereafter lead a carefree life?

Not necessarily! It takes, as the rest of this book will show, more than that.

But there is an answer. You definitely can see, dispute, and surrender the irrational ideas with which you upset yourself. You can use scientific thinking to uproot your self-defeating dogmas.

How?

Read the next chapter and see.

But first, an exercise.

RET Exercise No. 1

At first, the following exercise seems very simple, but it is not quite as easy as it appears. It gives you practice at distinguishing between your *appropriate* and your *in*appropriate negative feelings when you view something in your life as "unfortunate" or when you are concerned about a "bad" event occurring.

Distinguishing between appropriate concern, caution, vigilance and inappropriate anxiety, nervousness, and panic.

Imagine some very bad or unfortunate thing that might happen to you soon, such as losing a good job, being hurt in an accident, or losing a loved one. Vividly imagine that this event may easily occur. How do you feel? What are you telling yourself in order to create this feeling?

If you feel appropriate concern or caution, you are telling yourself something such as, "I certainly wouldn't like this unfortunate thing happening, but if it does occur, I can handle it." "If my mate were very ill or dead, that would be very sad, but I could still live and be reasonably happy." "If I lost my sight, that would be exceptionally handicapping, but I could still have a good many enjoyments."

Notice that all these thoughts state how deprived and sorry you would be if certain events occurred, but all add a *but* that would still leave you an option for living and enjoying life.

If you feel *in*appropriate anxiety, nervousness, or panic, look for these kinds of *musts, necessities, awfulizings, I-can't-stand-its, self-downings,* and *overgeneralizations:* "If I lost my job, as I *must* not, I could *never* get a good one again, and that would show what a wholly *incompetent person* I am!" "I must have a *guarantee* that my mate *must* not die, for if he or she did, I *couldn't stand* being alone and would *always* be miserable." "It's *absolutely necessary* that I not lose my sight, for if I did, my life would be *awful* and *horrible*, and I could never enjoy anything again!"

Note that these are predictions of unconditional and complete pain and that they leave you *no* way out of continual suffering.

Imagine, again, that something dreadful has actually happened to you, such as losing all your money, having a boss who is always criticizing you, or being treated very unfairly by your best friend or mate. Do you, as you imagine this, feel *only* sorry, sad, and regretful? Or do you *also* feel inappropriately depressed or angry?

If you feel depressed, look for *shoulds, oughts,* and *musts* like these: "I *should* have been more careful with my money. What a fool I was for not being more cautious!" "My boss *ought* not criticize me like that! I *can't bear* that kind of continual criticism!"

If you feel very angry, look for *mus*turbating self-statements like these: "My best friend *must* not treat me that unfairly! What a thorough louse he is!" "My living conditions *have* to be better than they are! How unjust and horrible it is that things are this way!"

Whenever you have strong negative feelings because unfortunate things are actually happening to you or you imagine that they might occur, see whether these feelings appropriately follow from your *wishes* and *desires* to have better things occur. Or are you creating them by going beyond your preferences and inventing powerful *shoulds, oughts, musts, demands, commands,* and *necessities*? If so, you are turning concern and caution into *over*concern, severe anxiety, and panic. Observe the real difference in your feelings!

CHAPTER 3

Can Scientific Thinking Remove Your Emotional Misery?

You can figure out by sheer logic that if you were only—and I mean *only*—to stay with your desires and preferences, and if you were never—and I mean *never*—to stray into unrealistic demands that your desires *have to* be fulfilled, you could very rarely disturb, *really* disturb, yourself about anything.

Why?

Because your preferences start off with, "I would very much *like* or *prefer* to have success, approval, or comfort," and then end with the conclusion, "*But* I don't *have* to have it. I won't die without it. And I could be happy (though not *as* happy) without it."

Or your preferences begin with, "I would distinctly *dislike* or *abhor* failure, rejection, or discomfort." They then conclude, "*But*, if I experience failure, rejection, or pain, I *can stand it*. I won't *collapse*. I can *still* be reasonably happy (though not *as* happy) if I have these unfortunate experiences."

When you insist, however, that you always *must* have or do something, you think in this way: "Because I would very much *like* or *prefer* to have success, approval, or pleasure, I absolutely, under practically all conditions, *must* have it. And if I don't get it, as I completely *must*, it's *awful*, I *can't stand it*, I am an *inferior person* for not arranging to get it, and the world is a *horrible place* for not giving me what I *must* have! I am sure that I'll *never* get it, and therefore I can't be happy *at all!*"

When you think in this rigid, *mus*turbatory way, you will frequently feel anxious, depressed, self-hating, hostile, and self-pitying. Just stick to your profound, rigid *shoulds*, *oughts*, and *musts* and you will see how you *feel*!

21

Are dogmatic and unconditional *musts* the only causes of emotional problems? No, not exactly. Some disturbances, such as psychosis and epilepsy, may include few *musts*. Other mental problems, such as severe depression and alcoholism, may involve physical ailments that actually create, as well as are created by, musts and other forms of crooked thinking.

But the usual kinds of emotional disturbances or neuroses (such as most feelings of anxiety and rage) largely come from grandiose thinking. Even when you have great feelings of inadequacy? Yes, your inferiority feelings are, ironically, the result of your godlike demands.

Take Stevie, for example. Twenty-three, with a law degree and well on his way to becoming a CPA, Stevie seemed to have everything anyone could want. Including a great build, almost perfect features, and adoring—and filthy rich—parents. Yet, Stevie was a social basket case—with no friends, no dates, unable to talk about anything but law and business. And he thoroughly hated himself.

Did Stevie have an older brother who was much better than he at socializing?

Was he unconsciously guilty about lusting after his mother?

Had he struck out on the ball field with three kids on base and been laughed at by all his sixth-grade classmates?

Did his father yell at him for masturbating and threaten to cut his penis off?

None of the above. Stevie had few childhood traumas and succeeded at almost everything he did.

But . . . ?

By the time he reached puberty, in spite of the love and acceptance of his parents, and in spite of his fine performance at school and at sports, Stevie hated himself.

Why?

Because he was lousy at conversation. He had a high-pitched voice and a slight lisp. And, perfectionist that he was, he demanded of himself that he speak beautifully. But the more he insisted that he had to speak very well, the more he stuttered and stammered. Then he mainly shut up and withdrew.

By the time he was twenty-three, everyone knew Stevie as an exceptionally shy, inhibited young man. No one doubted his self-hatred. But few realized his underlying grandiosity—his absolute need to be perfect and ideal in every respect and his complete refusal to accept any kind of mediocrity. Only after several months of RET was I able to show Stevie that he was laying many *shoulds* on himself. Such as: "I have to be great at *every* important thing. And when I talk stupidly or badly *at all*, as I absolutely *must not*, I am completely worthless. So why, when I cannot speak outstandingly well, try at all?"

At first, Stevie couldn't admit his perfectionism. But he finally saw his godlike demands on himself. Once he recognized these demands and began to use RET to dispute them, and once he began to feel that he didn't *have to* speak beautifully, he lost his feelings of inadequacy. Even though he still lisped and talked in a high-pitched voice, he stopped withdrawing, and forced himself to keep talking and talking—and finally became a good conversationalist.

Not all emotional disturbance stems from arrogant thinking. But most of it does. And when you demand that you *must* not have failings, you can also demand that you must not be neurotic. Stevie, for example, clearly saw that he was neurotic—and then put himself down for being disturbed and hence made himself *more* neurotic.

Thus, he told himself, "Other people aren't as shy as I am. How nutty of me to be so shy when most others don't have this problem. I must not be so neurotic! How stupid of me to be this disturbed!" So he created a secondary problem—a neurosis about his neurosis!

When you are neurotic, you almost always make yourself that way with illogical and unrealistic thinking. First, you are born with a talent for accepting and creating self-damaging ideas. Then you are considerably aided by your environment—which gives you real troubles (such as poverty, disease, and injustice) and which often encourages your rigid thinking (such as, "Since you have musical ability, you absolutely *ought* to be an outstanding musician").

But neurosis still comes mainly from *you*. You consciously or unconsciously *choose* to victimize yourself by it. And you *can* choose to stop your nonsense and to stubbornly refuse to make yourself neurotic about virtually anything.

You really *can*?

Yes, that is the main thrust of this book. You can think scientifically. As a brilliant psychologist, George Kelly, pointed out in 1955, you are a natural scientist. Thus, you *predict* what will happen if you decide to save money to buy a good car. And, once you decide, you *observe* the results of your decision and *check* them to try to *confirm* your predictions. Will you actually be able to save enough? Will you, if you do, get a good car? You check to see.

That is the essence of science: setting up plausible hypotheses or guesses and then experimenting and checking to uphold or disprove them. For a hypothesis is not a *fact*—only a guess, an assumption. And you check it to determine if it is correct. If it proves false, you reject it and try a new hypothesis. If it seems correct, you tentatively keep it—but always stand ready to change it if later evidence against it arises.

This is the scientific method. It is hardly infallible and often produces uncertain results. But it is probably the best method we have of discovering "truth" and of understanding "reality." Many mystics and religionists have argued that science gives us only a *limited* view of reality and that we can achieve Absolute Truth and Cosmic Understanding by pure intuition or direct experience of the central energy of the universe. Interesting theories—or hypotheses! But hardly as yet proved. And most likely we can never prove or disprove them. Therefore, they are not science.

Science is not merely the use of logic and facts to verify or falsify a theory. More important, it consists of continually revising and changing theories and trying to replace them with more valid ideas and more useful guesses. It is flexible rather than rigid, openminded instead of dogmatic. It strives for a greater truth but not for absolute and perfect truth (with a capital T!).[1]

The principles of RET outlined in this book uniquely hold that anti-scientific, irrational thinking is a main cause of emotional disturbance and that if RET persuades you to be an efficient scientist, you will know how to stubbornly refuse to make yourself miserable about practically anything. Yes, anything!

For if you are consistently scientific and flexible about your desires, preferences, and values, you will not escalate them into selfdefeating dogmas. You will then think, "I strongly prefer to have a fine career and be with a partner I love." But you will not fanatically—and unscientifically!—add: (1) "I *must* have a fine career!" (2) "I can *only* be happy with a partner I love!" (3) "I am a *thoroughly rotten person* if I don't achieve the fine career and great relationship I *must* achieve!"

RET also shows you that if you do, somehow, devoutly believe these rigid *musts* and thereby make yourself miserable, you can always use the scientific method to dispute and uproot them, and can start thinking sanely again. For that is what emotional health largely is—sane or scientific thinking. It is next to impossible, RET holds, to make and keep yourself seriously neurotic if you give up all dogma, all bigotry, all intolerance. For if you think scientifically, you can *accept*—though hardly *like*—unchangeable hassles and stop making them into "holy horrors."

Of course, you always *won't* do this. In no way!

You have as much chance to be a perfect scientist as you have, say, to be a perfect pianist or writer. As a very *fallible* human, you'll hardly reach perfection!

You can strive, if you wish, to be *as* good as you can be. But you'd better not try for perfection! You can *wish* for it, *prefer* to achieve it, and thereby refuse to upset yourself if you fall short. Even *desiring* real perfection seems futile. But to *demand* it seems—well, almost perfectly insane!

So even if you thoroughly read this book and energetically strive to follow its suggestions, you will not become a perfect scientist—or make yourself completely "unmiserable" for the rest of your life. To reap this kind of utopian harvest, try some devout cult which will promise you pure bliss forever. Science will not. But here is a more realistic RET plan:

To challenge your misery, try science. Give it a real chance. Work at thinking rationally, sticking to reality, checking your hypotheses about yourself, about other people, and about the world. Check them against the best observations and facts that you can find. Stop being a Pollyanna. Give up pie-in-the-sky. Uproot your easy-to-come-by wishful thinking. Ruthlessly rip up your childish prayers.

Yes, *rip them up*! Again—and again—and again!

Will the millennium then arrive? No. Will you never again feel disturbed? I doubt it. Will you reduce your anxiety, depression, and rage to near-zero? Probably not.

But I can, almost, just about promise you this: The more scientific, rational, and realistic you become, the less emotionally uptight you will be. Not zero uptight—for that is inhuman or superhuman. But a hell of a lot less. And, as your years go by, and your scientific outlook becomes more solid, less and less neurotic.

Is that a guarantee? No, but a prediction that will probably be fulfilled.

RET Exercise No. 2

Think of a time when you recently felt anxious about anything. What were you anxious or overconcerned about? Meeting new people? Doing well at work? Winning the approval of a person you liked? Passing a test or a course? Doing well at a job interview? Winning a game of tennis or chess? Getting into a good school? Learning that you do not have a serious disease? Being treated unfairly?

Look for your command or demand for success or approval that was creating your anxiety or overconcern. What was your *should, ought,* or *must*? Look for these kinds of anxiety-creating thoughts:

"I *must* impress these new people I am meeting."

"Because I *want* to do well at work, I *have* to!"

"Since I like this person very much, I've *got* to win his or her approval!"

"Passing this test or course is very important. Therefore, I *have* to pass it!"

"Because this looks like a good job, *it is necessary* that I please the interviewer."

"If I win this tennis (or chess) game, I will prove how good a player I am. Therefore, *it is essential* that I win it and show everyone that I'm really good!"

"This school that I've applied to is one of the best I could enter and I really want to get in it. Consequently, I *must* get accepted and it would be *horrible* if I didn't!"

"It would really be *terrible* if I had a serious disease and if I did I couldn't stand it. I *must* know for certain that I don't have it!"

"I treated these people very well and therefore they *must not* treat me unfairly and it would be *awful* if they did!"

In every instance where you have recently felt anxious and overconcerned, look for your preferences ("I would very much like to get this job") and then find your command or *must* ("Therefore, I *have* to get it and I *couldn't bear it* if I don't!").

Do the same for your recent feelings of depression. Find what you are depressed about, then persist till you find your *should, ought,* or *must* that is creating your depression. Examples:

"Because I want this job and *should have* prepared for the interview and didn't prepare as well as I *must*, I'm an *idiot* who doesn't *deserve* a good job like this!"

"I could have practiced more to win this tennis match but didn't practice as much as I *should* have, and that proves that I'm a lazy slob who will *never* be very good at tennis or anything else!"

Find your *shoulds*, *oughts*, and *musts* that recently made you feel quite angry at someone about some event. For example:

"After I went out of my way to lend John money, he never paid it back, as he absolutely *should* have! What an irresponsible louse he is! He *must* not treat me that way!"

"I could have gone to the beach on Saturday, but foolishly waited until Sunday—when it rained. The weather *should* have continued to be good on Sunday. How *horrible* it was that it rained. I *can't stand* rain when I want to go to the beach!"

Assume that every time you really feel anxious, depressed, or angry you are not only strongly *desiring* but also *commanding* that something go well and that you get what you want. *Cherchez le* should, *cherchez le* must! Look for your *should*, look for your *must*! Don't give up until you find it. If you have trouble finding it, seek the help of a friend, relative, or RET therapist who will help you find it. Persist!

CHAPTER 4

How to Think Scientifically About Yourself, Other People, and Your Life Conditions

Let us suppose that I have now sold you on using the scientific method to help yourself overcome your anxiety and to lead a happier existence. Now what? How can you specifically apply science to your relations with yourself, with others, and with the world around you?

Read on!

Science, as I pointed out in the previous chapter, is flexible and nondogmatic. It sticks to facts and to reality (which always can change) and to logical thinking (which does not contradict itself and hold two opposite views at the same time). But it also avoids rigid all-or-none and either/or thinking and sees that reality is often two-sided and includes contradictory events and characteristics.

Thus, in my relations with you, I am not a totally *good person* or a *bad person* but a *person who* sometimes treats you well and sometimes treats you badly. Instead of viewing world events in a rigid, absolute way, science assumes that such events, and especially human affairs, usually follow the laws of certainty.

The main rules of the scientific method are these:

1. We had better accept what is going on (WIGO) in the world as "reality," even when we don't like it and are trying to change it. We constantly observe and check "facts" to see whether they are still "true" or whether they have changed. We call our observing and checking reality the empirical method of science.

2. We state scientific laws, theories, and hypotheses in a logical, consistent way and avoid important, basic contradictions (as well as

29

false or unrealistic "facts"). We can change these theories when they are not supported by facts and by logic.

3. Science is flexible and nonrigid. It is skeptical of all ideas that hold that anything is absolutely, unconditionally, or certainly true—that is, true under all conditions for all time. It willingly revises and changes its theories as new information arises.

4. Science does not uphold any theories or views which cannot be falsified in some manner. For example, the idea that invisible, all-powerful devils exist and cause all the evils in the world. It doesn't claim that the supernatural does not exist, but since there is no way of proving that superhuman beings do or do not exist, it does not include them in the realm of science. Our *beliefs* in supernatural things are important and can be scientifically investigated, and we can often find natural explanations for "supernatural" events. But it is unlikely that we can ever prove or disprove the "reality" of superhuman beings.

5. Science is skeptical that the universe includes "deservingness" and "undeservingness" and that it deifies people (and things) for their "good" acts or damns them for their "bad" behavior. It does not have any absolute, universal standard of "good" and "bad" behavior and assumes that if any group sees certain deeds as "good" it will *tend to* (but doesn't *have to*) reward these who act that way and will *often* (but not *always*) penalize those who act "badly."

6. In regard to human affairs and conduct, science again does not have any absolute rules, but once people establish a standard or goal—such as remaining alive and living happily in social groups—science can study what people are like, the conditions under which they live, and the ways in which they usually act; and it can to some extent judge whether they are meeting those goals and whether it might be wise to modify them or to establish other ways to achieve them. In regard to emotional health and happiness, once people decide their goals and standards (which is not easy for them to do!), science can often help them achieve these aims. But it gives no guarantees! Science can tell us how we probably—but not *certainly*—can have a good life.

If these are some of the main rules of the scientific method, how can you follow them and thereby help yourself be emotionally healthier and happier?

Answer: By taking your emotional upsets, and the irrational Beliefs (iBs) that you mainly use to create them, and by using the scientific method to rip them up.

To show you how you can do this, let us take some common irrational commands and show how you can scientifically examine them.

Irrational Belief: "Because I strongly prefer to do so, I *must* act competently."

Scientific Analysis:

Is this belief realistic and factual? Obviously not. Because I am a human with some degree of choice, I don't *have to* act competently and can choose to act badly. Moreover, since I am *fallible*, even if I chose always to act competently, I clearly have no way of realistically doing so.

Is this belief logical? No, because my fallibility contradicts the demand that I *always* must act competently. Also, it doesn't logically follow, from my strong *preference* to do so, that I *have to* do so.

Is this belief flexible and unrigid? No, it says that under *all* conditions and in *all* ways, I must act competently. It is therefore an *un*flexible, rigid belief.

Can this belief be falsified? In one way, yes. Because I can prove that I do *not* have to behave competently at all times. But the belief that I *must* act competently implies that I am a supernatural god whose desire for competence must *always* be fulfilled and who has the power to fulfill it. There may be no way to fully falsify this godlike command, because even if I at times act incompetently, I can claim that I deliberately did so for some special reason and that I can always, if I will to do so, act competently. I can also say, "God's will be done!"—and that, as God, I don't have to explain why I acted "incompetently."

Does this belief prove deservingness? No, this again is an idea that cannot, except by fiat, be proven or disproven. I can legitimately hold that because I am intelligent and because I try hard, I will *usually* or *probably* act competently. But I cannot show that because of my intelligence, my hard work, my aliveness, my desire to succeed, or anything else, the universe undoubtedly *owes* me competence. That kind of obligation, deservingness, or necessity clearly doesn't exist—or else, once again, I *would* always be competent.

Does this belief show that I will act well and get good, happy results by holding it? Definitely not. If I act competently all the time, I may actually get bad results—because many people may be jealous of me, hate me, and try to harm me for being so perfect. And if I rigidly believe that "because I strongly prefer to do so, I *must* act competently," I will at times see that I do not act as well as I presumably must, and will therefore tend to hate myself and the world and make myself anxious and depressed. So this idea won't work—unless I somehow manage to always act quite competently!

Irrational Belief: "I *have to* be approved by people whom I find important, and it's *awful* and *catastrophic* if I am not!"

Scientific Analysis:

Is this belief realistic and factual? Clearly not, because there is no law of the universe that says that I *have to* be approved of by people whom I find important and there is a law of probability that says that many of the people I would prefer to approve of me definitely will not. It's not *awful* or *catastrophic* when I am not approved of, because only uncomfortable (but hardly dreadful) things will happen to me when I am not approved of. When something is "awful" it is (a) exceptionally bad; (b) totally bad; or (c) more than bad. Being disapproved of by important people may not even be exceptionally but only moderately bad. It is certainly not totally bad—for it could always be worse. And it cannot be more than bad, or 101 percent bad. So this belief doesn't by any means conform to reality.

Is this belief logical? No, for just because I find certain people important it does not follow that they *must* approve of me. And even if I find it highly inconvenient when important people do not approve of me, it doesn't follow that my life will be *catastrophic* or *awful*. Indeed, if someone I like does not quickly like me, I may actually gain: for this person might first like me and later frustrate or leave me.

Is this belief flexible and unrigid? Definitely not, because it holds that under *all* conditions and at *all* times people whom I find important absolutely have to approve of me. Quite inflexible!

Can this belief be falsified? Yes, because important people *can* disapprove of me and I can *still* find life desirable. But it also implies omniscience on my part, since I am *commanding* that people whom I find important must under all conditions approve of me; and even when they don't approve, I can *view* them as approving or contend that they really *do* approve, even when the facts show that they most probably don't. I can always claim that I *am* omniscient and that I know people's secret thoughts and feelings; and this kind of belief is unfalsifiable.

Does this belief prove deservingness? No, I cannot prove that even if I act nicely to important people that there is a rule of the universe that they *ought to* and *have to* approve of me. Deservingness is another unfalsifiable belief.

Does this belief show that I will act well and get good, happy results by holding it? On the contrary. No matter how hard I try to get people to approve of me, I can easily fail—and if I then think that they *have to* like me, I will most probably feel depressed. By holding the idea that at all times under all conditions people whom I find important *must* approve of me I will almost certainly fail to work effectively at getting their approval and also hate them, myself, and the world when they do not do what they supposedly *must*.

Irrational Belief: "People have to treat me considerately and fairly, and when they don't they are rotten individuals who deserve to be severely damned and punished."

Scientific Analysis:

Is this belief realistic and factual? No, it isn't. It commands that under all conditions and at all times other people have to treat me considerately and fairly. Obviously, they don't and the facts of life often prove that they won't. It is also not factual that they are rotten individuals—for such people would be rotten to the core, would never do good or neutral acts, and would be eternally doomed to act rottenly. No such *totally* rotten people seem to exist. This belief also implies that people who treat me inconsiderately and unfairly *always* deserve to be severely punished and that somehow their damnation and punishment *will be* arranged. This is not what happens in reality.

Is this belief logical? No, because it implies that because people sometimes do treat me inconsiderately and unfairly, they are totally rotten individuals and always deserve to be punished. Even if I can indubitably prove that, by usual human standards some people treat me badly, I cannot prove that *therefore* they are totally rotten and *therefore* always deserve to be punished. Such conclusions do not follow from my empirical observations that people treat me badly.

Is this belief flexible and unrigid? No, because it states and implies that in every single case *all* people who treat me inconsiderately and unfairly are *totally* rotten and *invariably* deserve to be severely damned and punished. No exceptions!

Can this belief be falsified? Part of it can be, because it holds that people who treat me badly and unjustly are totally rotten individuals and it can be shown they often do some good and neutral acts. My belief in deservingness and damnation, however, cannot be falsified, because even if no one else in the world upheld me and believed it to be true, I could always claim that all the other people in the world were sadly mistaken, that my view of punishment and damnation is unquestionably the right one, and that punishment for those who treat me unfairly *should* exist, even when it doesn't. When people who wrong me are, in fact, not severely punished, I can always contend that there are special reasons why they have not been penalized so far, and that they indubitably will be in the future or in some afterlife.

Does this belief system prove deservingness? No, even if people treat me inconsiderately and unfairly, and even when they sometimes are punished after they do so, I cannot prove that (1) they were punished *because* they treated me badly; (2) that some universal fate or being *dooms* them to this punishment; or (3) that hereafter they (and other people like them) will *always* be damned and doomed for treating me (and others) unjustly. I will even have trouble proving that their acts against me indubitably *are* bad—because in some respects they may be "good" and because some others may not view them as "bad." The concept of deservingness for one's "sins" implies that certain acts are unquestionably under all conditions "sinful." And this is impossible to prove.

Does having this belief mean that I will act well and get good, happy results by holding it? Not at all! If I strongly believe that people have to treat me considerately and fairly, that they are rotten individuals when they don't, and that they then deserve to be severely damned and punished, I will very likely bring on several unfortunate results: (1) I will feel very angry and vindictive, and will consequently stir up my nervous system and my body in a way that will often prove harmful to me. (2) I will be obsessed with the people who I think have done me in, and will spend enormous amounts of time and energy thinking about them. (3) When I try to do something about people's unfair acts, I will tend to be so enraged that I will fight with them in a frantic manner, and will often fail to convince them or stop them. Indeed, they are likely to see *me* as an overly enraged, and therefore unfair, person and to deliberately resist acknowledging their wrongdoing. They may even vindictively harm me further. (4) I will probably be unable to understand why people treat me "wrongly," may unjustly or paranoically accuse them of wrongs that they have not committed, and will often interfere with my amicably and objectively discussing with them and perhaps arranging for suitable compromises.

If you resort to scientifically questioning and challenging your own irrational Beliefs, as shown in the above examples, you will tend to see that they are unrealistic, distinctly illogical, often inflexible and rigid, they cannot be falsified, and are based on false concepts of universal deservingness. If you continue to hold these unrealistic and illogical notions, you will frequently sabotage your own interests.

This kind of analysis and disputing of your irrational Beliefs (iBs) is one of the main methods of RET. If you continue to use it, you will take advantage of the most powerful antidote to human misery that has so far been invented: scientific thinking. Science will not absolutely *guarantee* that you can stubbornly refuse to make yourself miserable about anything. But it will greatly help!

RET Exercise No. 3

Whenever you feel seriously upset (anxious, depressed, enraged, self-hating, or self-pitying), or are foolishly behaving against your own basic interest (avoiding what you had better do or addicted to acts that you'd better not do), assume that you are thinking unscientifically. Look for these common ways in which you (and practically all your friends and relatives) deny the rules of science:

Unrealistic thinking that denies the facts of life. Examples:

"If I am nice to people, they will surely love me and treat me well."

"If I don't pass this test, I'll never get through school and will end up as a bum or a bag lady."

Illogical and contradictory beliefs. Examples:

"Because I strongly want you to love me, you have to do so."

"When I fail at a job interview, that proves that I'm hopeless and will never get a good job."

"People must treat me fairly even when I am unkind and unjust to them."

Unprovable and unfalsifiable beliefs. Examples:

"Because I have harmed others, I am doomed to roast in hell and suffer for eternity."

"I am a special person who will always come out on top no matter what I do."

"I have a magical ability to make people do what I want them to do."

"Because I strongly feel that you hate me, it is certain that you do."

Beliefs in deservingness or undeservingness. Examples:

"Because I am a good person, I deserve to succeed in life and fate will make sure that nice things will happen to me."

"Because I have not done as well as I could, I deserve to suffer and get nowhere in life."

Assumptions that your strong beliefs (and the feelings that go with them) will bring good results and lead to comfort and happiness. Examples:

"Because you treated me unfairly, as you *should* not have done, my making myself angry at you will make you treat me better and make me happier."

"If I thoroughly condemn myself for acting stupidly, that will make me act better in the future."

When you have discovered some of your unscientific beliefs with which you are creating emotional problems and making yourself act against your own interests, use the scientific method to challenge and dispute them. Ask yourself:

Is this belief realistic? Is it opposed to the facts of life?

Is this belief logical? Is it contradictory to itself or to my other beliefs?

Can I prove this belief? Can I falsify it? Is there any sense in my holding it if it is unfalsifiable?

Does this belief prove that the universe has a law of deservingness or undeservingness? If I act well, do I completely deserve a good life, and if I act badly, do I totally deserve a bad existence?

If I continue to strongly hold the belief (and to have the feelings and do the acts which it often creates), will I perform well, get the results I want to get, and lead a happier life? Or will holding it tend to make me less happy?

Persist at using the scientific method of questioning and challenging your irrational Beliefs until you begin to give them up, increase your effectiveness, and enjoy yourself more.

CHAPTER 5

Why the Usual Kinds of Insight Won't Help You Overcome Your Emotional Problems

Will insight into your emotional problems help you overcome them? It may help—providing it is not conventional or psychoanalytic insight.

Conventional insight will help you very little. For it says that your knowledge of exactly how you got disturbed will make you less neurotic. Drivel! It will often help make you become nuttier!

Suppose, for example, that your parents insisted that you make a million dollars, else you are a slob. Suppose you have actually made little money and you now "therefore" feel worthless. Your wonderful "insight" about the "origin" of your self-hatred may only push you to loathe your parents. Or to hate yourself more for listening to them! Or to think that they were right—that you *should* have made a million dollars and are a turd for not following their great teachings.

Insight, even when it is correct, doesn't automatically *make* you better, though—if you *use* it correctly—it may help. And it can easily—very easily!—be false. For even if you did take your self-hating idea from your parents, we still had better ask: *Why* did you accept these ideas? What are you *now* doing to carry them on? How do we know that if your parents taught you to always accept yourself, you *still* wouldn't have concluded that you must make a million dollars to be worthwhile?

In other words, conventional "insight" is usually dubious and hardly tells you what factors *really* caused your disturbance. Nor what you can *do* to overcome it.

39

Psychoanalytic insight is worse. Because it is based on many different and contradictory guesses—and they cannot possibly all be true. Thus, if you now believe that you absolutely *must* make a million dollars to accept yourself, different analysts will try to convince you that you believe this because:

1. Your mother gave you pleasurable enemas and you are therefore "anally fixated" and are obsessed with money.
2. You unconsciously think that a bag of money represents your genitals and therefore your obsession with money really means that you want promiscuous sex.
3. Your father was cruel to you, so now you have to win his love and think you can do so only by making a million dollars.
4. You hate your father and want to shame him by making more money than he made.
5. You have a small penis or bosom and have to make lots of money to compensate for it.
6. Your unconscious views money as power and you really are obsessed with gaining power, not money.
7. Your great-grandfather was a pauper and you now have to remove the family shame about this by becoming a millionaire.

Et cetera, et cetera.[1]

All these psychoanalytic interpretations—and a thousand similar ones—are possible, but none of them is very plausible.[2] And even if one of these "insights" were true, how would knowing it help you *change* your obsession about making money?

If, for example, you truly think you have to win your father's love and that you can only do so by making a million dollars, how does that knowledge make you surrender your dire need for his approval? To change, you still would have to *dispute* that idea and to *act* against it. And psychoanalysis helps you do nothing like this—and encourages you (and your analyst) to keep looking for more brilliant "true" interpretations.

Conventional and psychoanalytic "insights," then, are not enough—or are too much. They frequently block scientific thinking and prevent active change. Does RET therefore ignore insight? Not at all! It uses—and teaches—several kinds of *un*conventional insight that help you understand your emotional problems, and what you can specifically *do* to uproot them.

In RET terms, insight first means understanding who you are. Actually, you *are* a human being who *has* various likes and dislikes and who *does* many acts to get more of what you like and less of what you dislike. So RET helps you explore your likes and dislikes and what you can do to achieve the former and avoid the latter.

RET, then, helps you not only to understand what you "are" but to *change* what you harmfully think, feel, and do. It accepts your desires, wishes, preferences, goals, and values, and tries to help you achieve them. But RET shows you how to separate your *preferences* from your *insistences*—and thus keep from sabotaging your own goals. It gives you insight into what you are now doing rather than into what you (and your damned parents!) have done.

Annabel, one of my clients who cherished her perfectionism because she felt that it made her a fine writer and an excellent mother, was having a hard time with some of David Burns's teachings against perfectionism in his book, *Feeling Good*. Dr. Burns, she thought, told her to give up all ideal goals and stick only to realistic and average ones. Then she couldn't be disappointed or depressed.

"But if I don't strive for ideal goals, I will never achieve half the good things I do achieve," she said. "How about *that*?"

"True," I replied, "you and many outstanding inventors and writers have striven for the ideal and have thereby helped yourself do remarkably well. RET, therefore, does not oppose competition or striving for outstanding achievement. It advocates *task*-perfection, but not *self*-perfection."

"What does that mean?"

"It means that you can try to be as good, or even as perfect, as you can—at any *project* or *task*. You can try to make *it* ideal. But *you* are not a good person if *it* is perfect. You are still a *person who* completed a perfect project, but never a *good person* for doing so."

"How, then, do I become an incompetent or bad person?"

"You don't! When you do incompetent or evil *acts*, you become a *person who acted badly*—never a *bad person*."

"But why, then, should I strive for perfection—or even for good achievements?"

"Because you presumably find *them*, the achievements, desirable. And if your achievements are outstanding or ideal, you will find them *more* desirable—more enjoyable. But your achievements, no matter how good, never make you a totally *good person*."

"But isn't Burns right about my being disappointed if I try for the ideal and don't reach it?"

"Yes—disappointed, but not self-hating if you use RET."

"And how do I do that?"

"By not giving up your *preference* for perfect motherhood or perfect writing, but eliminating your *demands*, or *musts*. As long as you tell yourself, 'I really would *like* to write a perfect novel—but I don't *have to*,' you'll retain your task-perfectionism but not your *self*-perfectionism."

"So the crucial difference is the *must*. I can strive for perfectionism in my writing as long as I don't think I *must* achieve it and do not view myself as a sleazy writer and a rotten person if I don't."

"Exactly!"

Annabel continued to work hard at perfecting her mothering and her writing. But she overcame the anxiety that drove her to therapy by changing her perfectionist *musts* back to *preferences*.

RET at times deals with your past—for if you are disturbed, you most likely had crooked thinking then as well as now. But it mainly shows what *you* did and what *you* thought in your early years—and spends little time on what your dear parents and others did to you. It especially shows you how you are *now* thinking, feeling, and acting—and how to *change* your weaknesses.

Insight, then, can help you see exactly how you are sabotaging yourself and what you can do to change. RET—which uses philosophy more than most other forms of therapy—stresses many different kinds of self-understanding. The following chapters will describe many insights that RET teaches and how you can use them in your efforts to stubbornly refuse to make yourself miserable about practically anything.

RET Exercise No. 4

Try to remember some of the worst incidents that took place during your childhood. How about the time your mother bawled you out in front of several of your friends? Or the time you were called upon to recite in class and were so panicked that you couldn't say anything and the whole class laughed at you. Or the time when your skirt or pants were hung too low and half of your behind was sticking out for everyone to see. Or the occasion when you told another child how much you really liked him or her and got only a cold or negative response.

Do you remember that very "traumatic" event or events? Do you still think that it greatly influenced the rest of your life?

Well, it really didn't! Not if you think about it carefully.

First of all, try to remember—or to figure out—what you told yourself to make this past event so "traumatic" and "hurtful." When your mother bawled you out in front of your friends, weren't you telling yourself that she *shouldn't* have done that and that you *couldn't stand* your friends' knowing something negative about you? When you were panicked about reciting in class, weren't you thinking, "I *must* answer my teacher well. Isn't it *awful* when I do poorly—and when the other kids laugh at me!" When you neglected to hitch up your skirt or pants and your behind was showing, weren't you telling yourself, "How shameful to be so careless about my clothing! I *must* not behave so foolishly!"

Track down—as you definitely can—the irrational Beliefs that *made* you feel hurt and upset when you were young. Then also look for the self-defeating ideas that you have *kept* repeating to yourself since that time and that have made you *keep* this "traumatic" incident alive.

Such as: "My own mother knew I was no good and that's why she kept criticizing me. She was right!" "I *still* can't recite well in front of people. How terrible!" "Because I dressed so sloppily as a child, everyone could see what a slob I was. And I still haven't improved, as I *should*. I am a fool who *deserves* to have others laugh at me!"

Use your knowledge of RET, and of how you upset yourself with your *musts* and commands, to understand exactly *how* you upset yourself during your childhood and how you are *still* preserving your upset feelings today.

CHAPTER 6

Insight No. 1: Making Yourself Fully Aware of Your Appropriate and Inappropriate Feelings

Insight is another name for awareness. Awareness is a first step toward ridding yourself of misery. The more you are keenly aware of your misery-creating thoughts, feelings, and behaviors, the greater your chances are of ridding yourself of them.

Let us—as we usually do in RET—start with your miserable feelings. How can you be aware of what you feel—and how appropriate your feelings are?

The first part of this question is fairly easy to answer: You know how you feel by merely asking yourself, "How do I feel?"

You sometimes may, of course, be defensive. You may deny that you feel anxious or angry because you are ashamed to admit such "wrong" feelings.

Usually, however, you won't. If you are severely anxious or depressed, you will tend to feel so uncomfortable that you will freely admit—at least to yourself!—that you have these miserable feelings. Such misery is easy to feel—and to acknowledge.

But how *appropriate* are your uncomfortable emotions? Oh, that's a much harder question to answer. But RET gives you a pretty good key. For it is the one system of psychotherapy that clearly distinguishes between appropriate and inappropriate feelings.

How? By stressing *Insight No. 1: You create both appropriate and inappropriate feelings when your goals and desires are blocked.*

You can—and had better—learn how to clearly distinguish be-

45

tween these self-induced emotional reactions. Most other
therapies—such as the behavior therapy of Joseph Wolpe and the
cognitive therapies of Richard Lazarus, Aaron Beck, and Donald
Meichenbaum—emphasize strong feelings, like severe sadness
and irritation, and put them into the same category as feelings of
depression and anger.[1]

Not so RET!

RET considers your strong feelings of sadness, irritation, and
concern healthy, because they help you to express your displea-
sure at undesirable happenings and to work at modifying them.
But RET defines your feelings of depression, anger, and anxiety as
(almost always) harmful, because they stem from your unrealistic
commands that unpleasant events absolutely *must* not exist, and
because they usually interfere with your changing these events
when they do exist.

Unlike most other therapies, therefore, RET shows you not only
how to get in touch with your negative (and your positive) feelings,
but also how to be aware of—to have *insight* into—whether they
are appropriate or *in*appropriate. It encourages you to feel your
feelings—and *also* to weigh how desirable they are. Do you really
want to feel them? And what good or bad results do they get you?

Thus, if you feel concerned about losing your job, you will try to
be on time, to work hard, and to cooperate with your boss and your
associates. If, however, you are *over*concerned—or severely
worried—about losing it, you will tend to be obsessed with it, *take
away* time and energy from doing it, and lose confidence that you
can perform it adequately.

Result? No damned job! Or a job and an ulcer. Or great misery
while working.

Again: If you are disappointed and regretful about being rejected
by a love partner, you will try to discover why you were abandoned, to win back that person's love, or to attempt to mate with a
more suitable partner. But if you are angry at your rejector, you
will probably antagonize him or her and remain an enemy instead
of a friend. And if you are depressed about being rejected, you will
tend to withdraw completely and see yourself as quite unlovable.

Your feelings of disappointment and regret, then, are usually *appropriate* feelings that help you withstand undesirable events and
strive for a happier future. Panic, depression, and rage, on the
other hand, are inappropriate feelings that interfere with your cop-

ing and block your improving of your life.

How about *mild* or *moderate* anxiety or anger? Don't *those* feelings spur you to act against life's hassles? Aren't *they* therefore beneficial?

Not exactly.

Almost any negative feeling occasionally can be useful. Extreme panic may energize you to outrun a forest fire. Intense rage may help you fight against an unfair bureaucracy.

May! But they probably won't!

Extreme panic will *usually* disorganize and freeze you so that you won't efficiently escape from the fire. Intense rage will *normally* make you *stew* instead of *do* when you encounter unfairness; and if you act while enraged you will often fight foolishly and badly.

You have, moreover, better choices. You can choose to be strongly concerned rather than grippingly panicked about escaping from a fire and you can decide to be greatly *displeased* and *determined to act against* unfairness.

With, most probably, better results! And with, almost certainly, less dreadful wear on your system!

RET holds that you can choose between great concern about your safety or panic or horror about it. And RET contends that you can decide to be strongly *displeased about* and *determined to change* injustice or rashly infuriated about it.

And you'd better be concerned about unpleasant happenings. For your feelings of concern, caution, care, and vigilance help keep you safe and satisfied; while your feelings of overconcern, anxiety, panic, and horror help keep you insecure and dissatisfied. Similarly, when you are treated unfairly or badly, you can choose to feel appropriately displeased, sorry, frustrated, and determined to change the unfair situation. Or you can choose to feel inappropriately angry, enraged, furious, and homicidal—and consequently whining and *in*active.

Can you clearly distinguish between inappropriate and appropriate feelings? Not always, since your emotions are rarely pure and often include appropriate and inappropriate elements. At one and the same time, you can be rationally *concerned* about escaping from a fire and irrationally *over*concerned or panicked about escaping. Where does the first feeling end and the second one begin?

RET has an answer. It holds that when you are appropriately

concerned about any danger, you are sensibly *desiring, wishing,* or *preferring* to avoid it. But when you are overconcerned, panicked, or horrified about the same danger, you are still desiring but *also* insisting that you absolutely *must*—yes, *have to*—avoid it. You *legitimately* and *wisely* desire to avoid danger. Because why should you not *want* what you want and why should you not *prefer* to avoid what you don't want?

No reason!

But your dogmatic command that you always *must* get what you desire is illegitimate and self-defeating—because the universe clearly does not *owe* you your heart's desire. And you will interfere with getting your preferences by fanatically demanding that they *have to be* fulfilled.

I have said that RET is more philosophic than other systems of psychotherapy. Now perhaps you can see how it is. When you are disturbed, RET's Insight No. 1 holds that you have both appropriate and inappropriate emotions. Usually (not always!) you can distinguish between the two by looking for the cognitions—the thoughts—that accompany them.

Your *appropriate* feelings arise from thoughts that express your preferences—such as, "I strongly *want* to avoid this fire but I don't *have to* escape and live happily ever after." And: "I abhor injustice and am determined to fight against it."

*In*appropriate feelings stem from *commanding, dictatorial,* thoughts—such as, "I *absolutely must* avoid this fire because the universe ordains that I *have to* live and be happy!" And: "I hate everyone who acts unjustly! They *absolutely must not* behave that way! At all costs, I *have to* stop them and make them see that they *must* always treat me fairly!"

Insight No. 1 of RET, once again, states: "You create both *appropriate* and *in*appropriate feelings when your goals and desires are blocked; and you can, and had better, learn how to clearly distinguish between these two self-created emotional reactions." By using the ABCs of RET—which are outlined in the next chapter—you can learn how to do this.

RET Exercise No. 5

Go back to the end of Chapter 2 and once again do the RET exercise that gives you practice in distinguishing between your appropriate and inappropriate negative feelings. Also try to see the difference between some of your appropriate and inappropriate positive feelings.

Imagine, for example, that you are performing something remarkably well—for example, playing tennis, or acting, or writing, or painting, or running a business in an outstanding manner. Let yourself feel very happy about this accomplishment.

Now observe your happy feeling. Is it only a feeling of being happy and pleased about *it*, your performance? Or do you also—be honest now!—feel great about *you*, about *yourself*, about your *whole being*? Do you feel like a *great person*—a noble, godlike, almost *superhuman individual*?

If you do feel like a noble, superhuman, holier-than-thou *person*, you are then, according to RET, experiencing an *in*appropriate positive feeling. For you are then in a grandiose, egotistical state and have raised yourself above other humans. You have jumped from the idea that "My behavior is outstanding" to "I am therefore an outstanding, great person!"

This is dangerous. Because when you *don't* perform remarkably well the next time, back to slobhood you will go! And even when you do perform well, you will be anxious about *not* doing so next time. So you had better like your fine *performance*—but not deify *yourself* for doing it.

When you do feel like a godlike, noble *person*, look for your *shoulds* and *musts*. Such as: "I have just done as well as I *have to* do. Good. My success makes me a fine, worthy individual." And: "Now that I have done this thing so well, people will see me as a marvelous person. I *need* them to see me in that light in order to accept myself and be happy with my life."

When you feel *in*appropriately bad or great, make a list of the disadvantages of having these feelings. You will find it easy to list the disadvantages of negative feelings, like those of depression, guilt or self-hatred. But your positive inappropriate feelings also have distinct disadvantages. Thus, when you feel like a great and superior *person*, here is a checklist of disadvantages which these feelings may bring you.

—Unrealistically assuming that you will always continue to perform well.

—Acting in an egotistical, arrogant, and obnoxious manner to others.

—Thinking that you are so great that you do not have to bother to work at performing well in the future.

—Being anxious about later falling on your face and greatly disappointing others who admire you.

—Maintaining and increasing your belief that you *have to* do well and that it is *terrible* if you don't.

—Making too much of the tasks at which you do well and neglecting other aspects of your life.

—Becoming so absorbed in your own ego that you lose your feelings for and understanding of others and ruin your human relationships.

—Striving so hard to continue to perform well that you put yourself under great stress and possibly interfere with your mental and physical health.

Ask yourself whether you are bringing on any of these—or other—disadvantages by making yourself feel inappropriate positive (or negative) feelings. If so, look again for the demands and commands with which you are creating these self-defeating feelings and work at disputing them and giving them up.

CHAPTER 7

Insight No. 2: You Control Your Emotional Destiny

Many modern therapies—particularly psychoanalysis—let people cop out on their responsibility for their own neuroses. Not RET. Over a decade ago, *Psychology Today* titled it, "The No-Cop-Out Therapy"—which indeed it is.[1]

Not that RET (like some extreme cults) says that you are *totally* responsible for your upsets. You aren't. As noted before, you are influenced by your biology and your learning, which also help you to become disturbed. Nonetheless!—you will, to *some* degree, control your emotional destiny. To *some* extent you choose how often and how intensely you upset your own emotional applecart. For you *listen* to your parents and teachers. You *carry on* their nonsense. You choose to *indulge* in your panic and despair—even when you sometimes know how to stop these feelings.

Yes—*you*.

Which is quite fortunate. For if emotional problems simply overwhelmed you, if outside conditions really *made* you as neurotic as you are, what could you do to help yourself be undisturbed? Damned little!

But if you, no one but you, mainly create your nervous destiny, you most likely can change this destiny. Whatever you *choose* to do, you can also *refuse* to do. Whatever you *choose* to think and feel, you can also *refuse* to think and feel. This is RET's *Insight No. 2: You largely (not completely) create your own disturbed thoughts and feelings; and therefore you have the power to control and change them. Providing that you accept this insight and work hard at using it!*

51

Let me outline the famous ABCs of RET. A stands for Activating Event—which is usually some happening that blocks or frustrates your important goals, desires, or preferences. For example: you want a job and you fail the interview and get rejected. A (Activating Event) is your failure and your rejection.

Please note! In RET, we start the ABCs of emotional disturbance with your goals, purposes, desires, and values. You *enter* these ABCs with (conscious and unconscious) Goals (G).

What, usually, are your main goals, about which you sometimes make yourself miserable?

They are, first, that you stay alive and, second, that you be satisfied or happy. Once you are born, you have strong biological tendencies to want to remain alive and to strive for contentment. If you didn't have the wish to survive, you rarely would. And if you didn't have the desire—the Goal—of being happy, you would probably not want to keep living. So your Goals of surviving and being happy while you are alive are inborn tendencies and help perpetuate you and your species.

How do you want to be happy or satisfied? In many ways, especially these:

When you are by yourself, alone.

When you are with other people.

When you are intimately involved with a few special people.

When you are doing well in business or a career and are earning a good living.

When you are involved in art, science, sports, or other recreations and creative acts.

Once you desire to survive and be happy, you bring these Goals to the ABCs of human living. You go to A (Activating Events) wishing, preferring to get your Goals fulfilled; and when you feel miserable and act foolishly (at point C, Consequences of A and B), your Goals are usually being blocked at A.

So now we have:

G—your Goal of getting what you want (especially, success and approval).

A—the Activating Events that block your Goal (especially, failure and rejection).

C—the Consequences of G and A (especially, feelings of anxiety and depression and self-defeating behaviors, like withdrawal and addiction).

Whenever your Goals (Gs) are thwarted by unfortunate Activating Events (As) and whenever you feel disturbed at Consequences (Cs), you tend to falsely blame C on A. Thus, you say, "Because I failed and got rejected at A and because I then felt depressed at C, A *causes* C. Failure and rejection *make me* depressed!"

Wrong!

False!

Mistaken!

A (failure or rejection that blocks your Goals) *contributes to* but never really *causes* C.

Why?

Because, obviously, if a hundred people with the same Goal (say, desire to obtain a job) all were blocked at A (got rejected), would they all feel equally depressed at C?

Obviously not.

Some would feel very depressed and suicidal. Some would feel disappointed and sorry but not really depressed. Some would feel relaxed or indifferent. A few would even feel happy. Why? Because these few would conclude that the job they wanted was really unpleasant. Or that they would rather be unemployed than be working.

So, you see, Activating Events (As) do *not* directly cause disturbed Consequences (Cs) in your gut—though they may contribute to these feelings.

This is not a new discovery of RET. Many philosophers have pointed this out—especially the Greek and Roman stoics, almost 2,500 years ago. One of their outstanding thinkers, Epictetus, put it very clearly in the first century A.D.: "People are disturbed not by things, but by the views they take of them." And Shakespeare restated this idea in *Hamlet*: "There's nothing either good or bad but thinking makes it so."

So RET's view of the ABCs of emotional disturbance has an honorable history. Not that RET—as you will see later—is pure stoicism. It isn't! But it agrees with Epictetus: You largely (not *entirely*) create your own misery. And you can *choose* not to do so.

How can you prevent and undo your upsetness? By gaining insight into the Bs in the ABCs of RET.

What are these Bs?

The Bs of RET are Beliefs. You can also call them cognitions, thoughts, views, opinions, values, meanings, attitudes, ideas, expectations, and philosophies. RET calls them Beliefs because they do appear to be beliefs. Other therapies use other names. But in this book we shall mainly use the term Beliefs.

You can be aware or unaware, conscious or unconscious of your Beliefs. You can express them in words, images, fantasies, symbols, and various other ways. If you would clearly understand and use them to change yourself, you had better state them consciously and verbally. But you can undo your misery-creating ideas in other ways, too. In fact, one of the virtues of RET is that it shows you *many* ways of changing your Beliefs—as I shall emphasize in this book.

When you needlessly make yourself miserable, you use two main kinds of Beliefs:

1. *Rational Beliefs (rBs)*. Your rBs are thoughts that help you feel appropriately and behave effectively—that enable you to get more of what you want and less of what you don't want. They include "cool" thoughts or calm descriptions of what is going on (WIGO) in your life. For example: "This job interviewer is frowning at me and may not favor me for this job." This is a "cool" thought because it tells you what the interviewer is doing but not how you *rate* or *evaluate* his or her act.

You can understand your feelings better if you look for the "warm" thoughts that you include in your rational Beliefs (rBs). For example: "Because I would like to get this job, I dislike this interviewer's frowning at me and wish he would stop frowning and instead beam at me." With these "warm" thoughts you express your desires, wishes, preferences, and dislikes. They *rate* or *evaluate* what is occurring in terms of your basic Goals (G).

"Warm" rational Beliefs are also undogmatic and are based on probability instead of certainty. For example: "There is a good chance that I would like this job if I get it, but I actually may not. And even if I would like it very much, I don't *have to* get it or keep rt—though it would be very nice if I did!"

2. *Irrational Beliefs (iBs).* Your iBs are thoughts that help you feel inappropriately and behave ineffectively—that interfere with your getting more of what you want and less of what you don't want. They start with "cool" thoughts ("This job interviewer seems to dislike me") as well as "warm" thoughts ("I wish he would like me and I hate his disliking me and keeping me from this job"). But they also include "hot" thoughts that strongly rate what is going on and are absolutist, dogmatic, and commanding. For example: "No matter what, I *must* have this interviewer like me and give me this job! If he doesn't, it's *awful!* I *can't stand it!* If I lose this job that proves that I am an incompetent, worthless person who will never be able to get and keep a good position!"

Note well! RET does not hold that *all* emotional disturbance stems from iBs, because it may have other important causes. Nor does it claim that all irrational Beliefs lead to disturbance, because (as John Dewey once said) many of them don't. You may irrationally believe, for example, that all women are crazy, that eating turtles will cure warts, and that two and two equal five, and you may not feel miserable. You will probably act inefficiently if you believe these (and a hundred other) irrational Beliefs. But you may or may not disturb yourself by holding them.

RET merely—and uniquely—contends that when you rigidly hold certain irrational Beliefs—when you dogmatically command that you *must* do well, *have to* be approved by others, *have got to* have people treat you fairly, and always *ought* to live with easy and enjoyable conditions—when you stoutly hold these iBs, you will tend to make yourself needlessly miserable and will probably defeat some of your most cherished goals.

RET further states that when you hold irrational Beliefs (iBs), you consciously or unconsciously *choose* these absolutist shoulds, oughts, and musts—and therefore you have the ability to consciously explore and change them. Let me therefore repeat *Insight No. 2:*

You largely (not completely) create and control your own disturbed thoughts and feelings; and therefore you have the power to radically change them. Providing that you accept this insight and work hard at using it!

More specifically: You can undo your misery *if* you work at
finding and surrendering your irrational Beliefs.

George, who had heard that RET deals with irrational Beliefs,
came to see me because he "irrationally" lusted after almost every
woman under forty that he met. George was twenty-five.

I soon showed George that he mainly had a strong *preference* for
sex with many women—but that was hardly irrational, as long as it
was only that, a preference. His rational Belief (rB) was: "I like sex
very much and I wish I could have it with most of the women I
meet."

His main irrational Belief (iB) was, "I *must* not have such a
strong sex preference! I *should* always be more selective in my
lusting—and only want to go to bed with women whom I really
like."

"Why is this belief irrational?" George asked me when he acknowledged having it.

"Because," I answered, "it's a command rather than a desire.
You can rationally prefer to have less desire—even to be without
any lust. But once you say to yourself, 'I *must* not desire! I *must* not
lust!' you will become obsessed with your desire—and probably experience it more intensely. Moreover, you will not be able to plot
and scheme how to diminish it. So your *determination* to be less
lustful may be okay. But your absolute *necessity* to be less lustful
will get you into trouble. It will tend to make you anxious and
guilty."

"It does!" George exclaimed.

"So you'd better see what your irrational Belief really is," I
pointed out.

"You mean," said George, "I have an irrational Belief about a
rational Belief—about my strong preference for sex. Is that right?"

"Very well put! In RET terms, you have an rB about an iB. Now
if we can help you to give up your irrational Belief that you *must*
not be lustful, you will still have the rational Belief that sex can be
very enjoyable, and will probably be able to engage in more sex—
and enjoy it thoroughly!"

"I see!" said George.

But although it was easy for him, with my help, to see the difference between his rB and his iB, he at first had trouble eliminating
the latter. For he correctly asked himself, at D (Disputing of irrational Beliefs), "Why *must* I not lust after many women? Why is it
wrong for me to do so?" And he correctly answered, "It's okay for

me to have strong sex drives. Therefore, I'm okay as a person."

This was a wrong answer because he soon went back to thinking. "But suppose it *is* wrong for me to be so sexy? Other men aren't as hungry as I am. So maybe I'm abnormal in that respect. And if I am, that makes me a pretty lousy person!"

When George came up with this answer—and still remained anxious and guilty—I showed him that he had a highly inelegant solution to his guilt problem and that a more elegant RET solution would be for him *first* to show himself that his preference, "I would like to have sex with many women," was rational. But second, he had better also understand that even if his sex desires were unusual, and if too much indulgence in them was irrational, that would only mean that he was a *person who* had "abnormal" desires but not an *"abnormal" or lousy person.* For RET shows people how to stop damning and to fully accept *themselves* even when some of their acts are stupid, wrong, or immoral.

Anyway, when George saw the difference between his rational and irrational Beliefs and when he kept working to surrender the latter, he finally became unanxious and unguilty about his strong sex drives. And one time, when he foolishly spent several weeks compulsively having sex with several women while sadly neglecting his retail business, he was able to conclude that his behavior was stupid and self-defeating but that he was not a *stupid, rotten person.* After that, he was able to handle his promiscuous desires more reasonably.

By understanding—and working at—Insight No. 2, George was able to control his emotional destiny. And sometimes to feel sorry but not depressed.

RET Exercise No. 6

Try to remember a recent time in which you felt anxious about something—such as feeling anxious or panicked about taking a test, playing in an important game, or asking for a promotion or a raise at work. Assume that you created this anxious feeling by thinking (1) a rational Belief (rB) or *preference*, and (2) an irrational Belief (iB) or strong *demand.*

Example of your rB or *preference*: "I would very much like to pass this test, but if I don't I can try to pass it later. And if I never pass it, I still can live and be happy."

Example of your iB or *demand*: "I have to pass this test, and if I don't I'll be a truly stupid person who will *never* be able to get what I really want."

Think, now, of a recent time when you felt depressed about a failure or a rejection. Assume, again, that you created this depressed feeling by telling yourself rational Beliefs (rBs) and irrational Beliefs (iBs). Find them!

Example of your rB or *preference*: "I strongly wanted to win that game but I can accept losing it and learn to play better next time. I can also enjoy playing even if I lose many games."

Example of your iB or *demand*: "I absolutely *ought to* have won that game and because I lost it I am a thoroughly rotten player and an incompetent person."

Think of a time when you became angry or enraged. Assume, once again, that you *made yourself* angry by holding both a rational Belief (rb) or *preference* and an irrational Belief (iB) or *godlike command*.

Example of your rB or *preference*: "I would have very much liked my boss seeing that I deserved a raise and giving me a good one. Since he didn't, he unfortunately doesn't appreciate my work and that's too bad, but hardly the end of the world."

Example of your iB or *godlike command*: "Because I am a good worker, my boss absolutely *should have* appreciated me and given me a good raise. Since he didn't, he's no damned good and deserves to lose his rotten business!"

Keep looking for and persist until you find your rational Beliefs (rBs) and irrational Beliefs (iBs) whenever you feel really anxious, depressed, enraged, self-downing, and self-pitying. Try to see that your rBs just about always express your preferences and distastes—what you want and don't want—and that your iBs express your unconditional musts, shoulds, and oughts—your godlike demands and commands on yourself, or others, and on the universe. Practice seeing this difference many times until you easily and automatically tend to clearly see it. Work at fully accepting the reality that however legitimate and appropriate your goals and wishes are, they are hardly the same as your dogmatic and needless demands.

CHAPTER 8

Insight No. 3: The Tyranny of the Shoulds

What main specific irrational Beliefs (iBs) do you use to upset yourself? You probably adopt and invent many of them, as we shall keep revealing in this book.

Your most important irrational pathway is *mus*turbation—or your devoutly following of what Karen Horney called "the tyranny of the shoulds."[1]

Following Horney's lead, we arrive at *Insight No. 3: You mainly make yourself needlessly and neurotically miserable by strongly holding absolutist irrational Beliefs (iBs), especially by rigidly believing unconditional shoulds, oughts, and musts.*

How do you acquire or invent your destructive musts?

Very easily!

As a human, you are first of all born suggestible—gullible—to the commandments of your parents and your culture. Worse yet, you have your own genius for inventing rules and regulations that you rigidly believe that you (and others) *have to* follow.

You, like virtually all humans, are a natural-born reasoner and problem solver. But you are also a master of rationalization, self-delusion, and bigotry.

You think straightly—and crookedly. In fact, you are sane enough to keep yourself alive and happy—and you are crazy enough to be very irrational, illogical, and inconsistent. As the long history of humanity clearly shows![2]

You so easily think foolishly that your thoughts often bring on emotional problems. I described twelve major irrational beliefs in my first paper on Rational-Emotive Therapy (RET) that I gave in

1956 at the American Psychological Association's Annual Convention in Chicago.[3]

Psychologists soon became so enthusiastic about these irrational Beliefs (iBs) that they devised several tests of irrationality and have now published hundreds of studies using these texts. Over ninety percent of these studies support the RET theory that emotionally disturbed people subscribe to more irrational ideas than do less disturbed individuals.[4]

Following my lead, a number of other therapists created tests of crooked thinking (such as the Beck Depression Inventory) which have been used in hundreds of research studies. Again, the results almost always show that disturbed people subscribe to more unrealistic and dogmatic thoughts than do less upset individuals.[5]

This widespread interest in irrational ideas has had some bad as well as good results. For humans create many kinds—perhaps hundreds—of irrationalities, which tend to influence their feelings and make them act inefficiently. But not all of these irrationalities, by any means, lead to neurosis.

If you believe that you are a good poker player when you really are not, you will probably foolishly risk playing with good players—and will often lose. If, however, you irrationally believe that you *must* be a great poker player and that you *have to* continually show others how good you are, you then probably will compulsively gamble, and keep gambling even when you steadily lose.

After I described the first twelve basic iBs of RET in 1956, I continued to explore my clients' irrationalities. To my surprise, I discovered that I could condense my original list into three main iBs—and that these were all *musts* instead of *preferences*. The three basic *musts* that create emotional problems are:

1. "*I* must perform well and/or win the approval of important people or else *I* am an *inadequate person!*"
2. "*You* must treat me fairly and considerately and not unduly frustrate me or else *you* are a rotten individual!"
3. "My life conditions *must* give me the things I want and *have to* have to keep me from harm or else *life* is unbearable and I *can't* be happy at all!"

As I boiled down the previous irrational ideas I had discovered into these three major *musts*, I also found that my clients' other upsetting beliefs were not independent but were consciously or unconsciously derived from their musts.

Take, for example, one of the most popular iBs, which I have named *awfulizing* or *horribleizing*: "It's *awful* if I fail at this important task and it's *horrible* if people reject me for failing."

This is a crazy idea, because although it may be highly *unfortunate* for you to fail and very *inconvenient* for you to be rejected, when you call failure and rejection *awful* and *horrible* you view them as *more than* bad or 101 percent inconvenient—which of course, they cannot be. They aren't even 100 percent bad— because they could even be *worse*. When you overgeneralize and go *beyond* reality in this way, you will make yourself feel panicked and depressed (instead of appropriately sorry and frustrated) if you fail and get rejected.

Now *why* does a bright person like you resort to this kind of silly, unrealistic awfulizing?

Mainly, I contend, because you start with a conscious or unconscious *must* and *then* you easily and "logically" derive your awfulizing from it. Thus, you start with "I absolutely *must* perform this task well!" Then you "reasonably" conclude, "And since I didn't perform as well as I absolutely *must*, it's *awful*, it's *more than* inconvenient, it's as bad *as it possibly could be*, it's the *end of the world*!"

If you *only* stayed with your *preference* for doing well and *never* escalated it into a *dire necessity*, a *must*, would you awfulize about your poor performance? Hardly ever! I contend. For your preference statement would be, "I would *like to* perform this task well but I don't ever *have to*. So if I fail, too bad—but not awful!"

Take another set of iBs: personalizing and all-or-none thinking: "Now that the person I truly love has rejected me, I'm sure I *acted very badly*. Therefore, I am a thoroughly *inadequate person* who will *always* be rejected and *never* be loved by someone for whom I care."

These ideas are irrational and self-defeating because:

1. You may not have acted badly at all and still may have been rejected because the person you love has peculiar tastes or prejudices. In fact, you may act so well that your beloved may conclude

that you are *too good* and that therefore he or she had better reject you before you later do the rejecting.

2. Even if you act badly with your beloved and therefore get rejected, you are hardly an *inadequate* person but a *person who* acted inadequately *this time* and who can learn to act better in the future.

3. Just because you get rejected now doesn't prove that you'll *always* be rejected and *never* be accepted by everyone for whom you care. If you keep trying, that's most improbable. Your conclusion is a silly overgeneralization.

Now why, again, does a reasonable person like you make such crazy conclusions?

Not because you simply *want* to be accepted. For then you would conclude that it's undesirable when you are rejected and would keep trying for future approval. You might possibly criticize your *efforts* but hardly damn *yourself* when a loved one rejects you.

But suppose you irrationally begin with strong and devout *musts*—such as, "I *must* win the love of everyone I truly love and must *never* be rejected!" You will then *easily* and *naturally* conclude, "Because I have been rejected, as I *must* not be, I am sure I acted badly and am an *inadequate person* who will *never* be loved the way I *must* be!"

RET, then, shows how you upset yourself with absolutistic shoulds, oughts, and musts. It holds that you can nicely hold *conditional* and *logical* musts—such as, "If I want to read this book, I must buy or borrow a copy." And: "If I want to get a degree at college, I must get passing marks in my required subjects." For these conventional musts merely say, "*If* I want something, then I *have to* act properly to get it. This kind of *must* is (though not always) realistic and helps you to act sensibly.

RET accepts your realistic *musts* but shows you how to look for your *un*conditional and *il*logical musts. Such as: "Even if I can't get a copy of this book, I still *must* read it." And: "Although I have not passed any college courses, because I strongly want a degree they *should* give it to me!"

RET adds this rule to Insight No. 3: In seeking to discover the irrational Beliefs (iBs) you use to disturb yourself, *cherchez le* should, *cherchez le* must! *Look for your dogmatic shoulds and musts!*

Using RET, you can quickly find these musts and see how you needlessly upset yourself by devoutly holding them. If you look! One of my clients, Sandra, insisted that she first felt that being rejected by a lover was *awful* and *terrible*, and that once she felt that way, she *then* said that she *must* not get rejected. To begin with, she insisted, she only had strong *desires*, and not *demands*, to be loved.

I was quite skeptical. "Let's suppose," I said, "you *only* wanted your lover strongly, and were not *also* insisting that you *must* not lose him. What would your entire belief be about having and losing him?"

"Uh—. I guess, I strongly *want* him to love me. And if he doesn't, that's *terrible* and I *can't stand it!*"

"You're implying that if you only *weakly* wanted him to love you and if he didn't, that would be somewhat *inconvenient* but hardly terrible. Right?"

"Yes, Only when I see that my strong desire for him may be blocked do I feel that it's terrible."

"But suppose you believed, 'I strongly *want* my lover to love me but he really doesn't *have to*. I really don't *need* him to love me, though I truly *desire* him to do so.' How would you *then* feel if you lost him?"

"Well—uh—if I really believed he didn't *have to* love me, that I don't *need* him to, I guess I would feel that I could go on without him and it wouldn't be so terrible. But it would be quite frustrating and bad."

"See! If you were not making his loving you a *necessity* but only a *strong desire*, you would feel highly *frustrated* and *inconvenienced*. The stronger your desire for his love is, the *more* inconvenienced you will be. But to turn your great inconvenience into a *holy horror*, to make it *terrible*, you are really adding a second idea: 'Since losing my lover is *so* bad, I *must* not be *that* inconvenienced. And if I am so *very* frustrated, as I *must* not be, that is *awful*, that is terrible!"

"So my *awfulizing* about losing my lover really stems from my *must*urbating about such a *great* loss?"

"Doesn't it? If you *only* stayed with a preference sentence, wouldn't you be saying to yourself, 'I hate like hell losing my lover.

But there is still no reason why I *must* not lose him'?"

"Yes, I guess I would."

"And would you not then conclude, 'Because there is no reason why I *must* not lose him, it would be highly obnoxious if I did, but the world won't come to an end, it won't be *terrible*, and I could still be a happy—though a less happy—person'?"

"Yes, I might well conclude that."

"I think you would! Your *awfulizing* and *terribleizing* basically stems from your *command*, *your necessity*, that this very bad loss *must* not occur."

"If I tell myself, 'Losing him is *awful!*' am I then saying that this loss *must* not exist?"

"Not always. You may just be using *awful* when you really mean, 'It's *very bad* losing him,' and that would merely make you feel appropriately sad and frustrated at this loss. But when you say to yourself, 'It's awful *that* I lost him,' you may also mean, 'It's *more than* bad, it *must not be* that bad, I *can't bear* that degree of badness!' Your *must* is crucial here. For missing out on your strong desire to be loved may indeed be *very* bad, and may help you feel *quite* sorrowful. But telling yourself that this degree of badness *absolutely ought not* exist and therefore is *more than* bad puts you outside of reality and makes you severely anxious and depressed. Do you see the difference?"

"I think I do. But it's hard to see it clearly and keep seeing it."

"True! Moreover, once you say to yourself, 'I *must* not lose my lover, and it would be *terrible* if I did,' you then tend to add, in a circular fashion, 'And since it would be so *terrible*, this loss *must not* occur, absolutely *should not* exist!' And then you foolishly think that your *musts* stem from your *terribleizing*."

"When only the *second* must does! Is that what you mean?"

"Yes. You *bring musts or demands* to the possible loss of your lover. You therefore define this loss as *terrible*. Then you *bring* the demand that 'terrible things *must* not exist!' to your terribleizing. So you have first-level and second-level *musts* which you tend to bring to undesirable situations. And you therefore have, very often, primary and secondary disturbances."

"Both of which I *make* exist because I tell myself that bad and 'horrible' things *must* not happen to me."

"Yes, that's a good point you're making. You can think that mildly bad, very bad, and so-called terrible events *must* not occur.

And in all these cases, even with the mildly bad events, you'll needlessly disturb yourself. While if you convince yourself that even the very worst things in life—such as painful deaths—*should* and *must* at times exist, because they simply and truly *do* exist, then you'll tend to feel sad and frustrated, but *not* severely anxious and depressed."

"I see now that the *must* seems to be basic to my disturbances," said Sandra.

"Fine. But don't let me talk you into this. Figure it out for yourself. Whenever you really feel miserable—especially panicked, depressed, or enraged—look for your *should*, look for your *must*. And then see that if you give it up, you'll still feel frustrated and saddened—but not off the wall!"

"Okay, I'll really keep looking."

Sandra did keep looking for her *musts and shoulds*—as well as for the *awfulizing* and *terribleizing* which stemmed from them—and for the first time in her life managed to feel quite sad but not depressed when an important lover rejected her. When she occasionally sank into depression again, she saw she had returned to *mustur*bation, worked at giving it up, and then felt alone and sad but not self-downing or depressed.

RET Exercise No. 7

Look for something that you really believe is *awful*, *terrible*, or *horrible*. See if you can find—as you most probably can—the *must* that lurks behind your defining this thing or act as *awful*.

Examples: "I think that being rejected by a person I truly love is *awful*."

Hidden musts:

". . . Because I *must* not be rejected by anyone I truly love."

". . . Because I *must* be good enough to win the favor of anyone I truly love."

". . . Because I *must* not be deprived of the companionship of someone I really love."

". . . Because I am a nice person who *deserves* to be loved, and therefore the world *must* arrange things so that I get the love I truly deserve!"

Look for something you think you *can't stand* and try to discover some of the *musts* that make you feel that you *can't stand* this thing.

Example: "The conditions under which I work are so disorganized and unfair that I *can't stand* working there."

Hidden musts:

"The conditions under which I work are so disorganized and unfair that they *must* not exist. And therefore I *can't stand* their being as bad as they *must* not be."

"I *must* have pleasure and relaxation at work, and I cannot have this when the conditions there are so disorganized and unfair. Therefore, these conditions are so bad that I *can't stand* them."

"I *must* have *some degree* of happiness at work and the conditions there are so disorganized and unfair that I can't be happy *at all* there. Therefore, I *can't stand* working there."

"My work *must* be the way I want it to be and the disorganized and unfair conditions where I work don't allow this. Therefore, I *can't stand* working there."

Look for some occasion when you felt you were an inadequate person, or felt worthless, or felt undeserving of good things. Try to discover your hidden musts that made you feel this way.

Example: "I failed a good many times to establish a long-term relationship with someone for whom I really cared. That shows what an inadequate, unlovable person I am."

Hidden musts:

"I *must* succeed in at least one long-term relationship, otherwise I am an inadequate, unlovable person."

"I *must* not *keep* failing at relationships with people for whom I care, and if I do I am clearly worthless."

"Because having a good relationship is the most important thing for me, I *have to* achieve one soon. If I fail at this, as I *must* not, I am obviously an inferior, undeserving person."

"I am *sometimes* allowed to fail at long-term relationships but I have failed *too many* times, as I *must* not! Failing so *many times* shows that I am an inadequate, unlovable person!"

Look for some time when you felt hopeless, and knew you would *never* succeed in life, and would *always* be deprived of what you most wanted. Find your hidden musts that led you to this feeling of hopelessness.

Example: "Now that I have lost several good jobs, I'll *never* be able to get and keep a good one, and *always* will be doomed to a lousy position."

Hidden musts:

"I *must* never keep losing good jobs, and if I do, I'll clearly *never* be able to get and keep a good one."

"I *have to* stay on a good job for a reasonable length of time. Otherwise, I'll *never* be able to get another good one and *always* be doomed to poor ones."

"I *must* prove what a worthwhile worker and person I am and will never be worthwhile if I keep losing good jobs. Being worthless, I'll never be able to get and keep a good job!"

"I can lose a good job now and then but *must* not keep losing so many of them. Since I keep losing them, as I *must* not, I'll *never* be able to keep a good one and *always* will be doomed to a lousy position."

Whenever you are upset about anything, look for your obvious or hidden dogmatic *musts*. Assume that you really have them; and if you can't find them ask a friend, relative, or therapist to help you look for them. *Cherchez le* should, *cherchez le* must. Seek and ye shall find!

CHAPTER 9

Insight No. 4: Forget Your "Godawful" Past!

For several years I was a highly successful psychoanalyst and thought that I was greatly helping my clients by exploring the gory details of their early life and showing them how these experiences made them disturbed—and how they could now understand and remove these early influences.

How wrong I was!

After I honestly admitted that my psychoanalytic "cures" were hardly as good as I would have liked them to be, I began to see that helping people to understand their past was not only doing them little good but was actually blocking their dealing with their *present* problems. So I founded RET and began to keep my clients in the present and to help them with their current difficulties. I immediately got much better results in teaching them how to be "unneurotic."

Many of my clients, however, still insisted on talking about their past—partly because they previously had years of psychoanalysis and had been trained to do so. I then showed them that, yes, their mother or brother had severely criticized them during their childhood (at point A, or Activating Event, in the ABCs of RET). And, yes, they had then undoubtedly felt depressed and self-downing (at point C, or Consequence). But A did *not* cause or create (though it may well have contributed to) C.

B (their Belief System) was the main contributor to C; and B included a rational Belief (rB)—such as, "I don't like being criticized. Maybe it shows that I'm doing something wrong and, if so, I'd better correct it." But B also included an irrational Belief (iB)—such as, "I *need* my mother's love and absolutely *must not* act badly and get her disapproval. If she, whom I *need*, dislikes me, I am surely an unlovable, crummy person!"[1]

So I showed my early RET clients the iBs that they *brought* to their early childhood situations. I proved to them that, as children, they basically *upset themselves*.

More important, I demonstrated by examining their present lives, how they were *still* using these same early iBs to castigate themselves and that they were *therefore* currently disturbed. Unlike many other people who were upset during childhood but long since *changed* their thinking and got over downing themselves (and hating their parents), these clients still actively *clung* to their original shoulds and musts, and refused to give them up.

Their early thoughts and feelings did not *make them* anxious today. Rather, their *present* and *continuing* dogmas (iBs) were really the more direct cause of their current neurosis.

This brings us to *Insight No. 4 of RET: Your early childhood experiences and your past conditioning did not originally make you disturbed. You did.*

You chose, because of your distorted thinking, to overreact or underreact to the Activating Events and Experiences of the past. You were actually an integral *part* of these Experiences.

Because when you do something (say, take a boat trip), you approach the situation (the boat, the people on it, the water on which it sails), and you *react*, as only *you* can react, to it. Moreover, you bring your memories of past events (including your reactions to these events) to the new situation, and you therefore "experience" it in a biased manner. You largely (though not completely) *are* your experiences—are an active creator of them.

So to some extent you "invented" your past. And when "it" supposedly "makes you" feel upset today, you are really choosing to keep it alive. How?

1. By thinking the same kind of irrational Beliefs (iBs) with which you upset yourself—during your childhood. For example, "I not only *want* my mother's approval but I completely *need* it and am a *basket case* without it!"

2. By still actively *holding on to* these views today.

3. By refusing to rethink and act against your iBs until you no longer use them to upset yourself.

In the past, you largely *made* your bed of neurosis and you are *insisting* on lying in it today! If, therefore, you use RET to understand your early life, you can focus on *your* part in creating it and on how *you* now perpetuate your childish thoughts, feelings, and behaviors.

Ironically, if you forget about your past, if you assume that you are still bothering yourself *today*, and if you look for what you are *now* doing to make yourself miserable, you will often see what *really* "happened" in your childhood—and what you did to *make it happen*. The less you gripe about your past, the more you tend to admit that you partly created it. The more you explore what you are *now* doing to cause your upset feelings, the more insight you will have.

Karen, a member of one of my regular therapy groups at the Institute for Rational-Emotive Therapy in New York, kept insisting that she hated herself because her mother continually told her, all during her childhood, that she was stupid and ugly. Rob, another group member, backed her up by stoutly contending that he had no confidence in himself because his father insisted that he become a wealthy businessman, and he actually turned out to be a low-paid civil servant.

The other group members and I tried to show Karen and Rob that their brothers and sisters, who had also been severely put down by their parents, were—peculiarly enough!—confident and self-accepting. No sale. Karen and Rob firmly held onto their "traumatic" pasts—and did little to change themselves in the present.

Audrey, a very attractive dentist, who had loathed herself all her life and was still shy and unassertive, finally spoke up: "I'm sick and tired of the two of you moaning and wailing about your goddamned parents and how they made you the way you are. Let me tell you about my mother and father. They were the nicest and most gentle people I ever met. They loved me and supported me in every which way. They always told me I was bright and beautiful and that they knew I could do anything I wanted to do. They treated my brother equally well; and he was, and still is, very kind to me. Well, as a result of all this marvelous upbringing, you know what a basket case I now am—as meek and self-hating as I possibly could be! So why don't both of you stop your shrieking about your horrible childhood and get on with your *present* lives? Just as I have to do about mine—in spite of my wonderful upbringing!"

Three other members of the group joined Audrey in affirming that they, too, had had fine, loving parents—and still hated themselves. One of them, Jose, said: "I now see, through RET, that I brought my perfectionistic *self* to my tolerant mother and father. No matter how often *they* accepted me, *I* pigheadedly refused to do so. And I *still* often refuse! So I keep working to change *me* and *my* perfectionism. As you two had better do also!"

Surprised by the group's reaction, Karen and Rob were taken aback. Karen did some more thinking, worked hard at accepting herself with her failings, and then was able to forgive her mother and have a good relationship with her. Rob temporarily stopped resenting his father but then went back to blaming him again for all his present problems. He quit the group, has been in psychoanalysis for the past five years, and according to one of his friends who regularly attends my Friday night workshops, still spends most of his therapy sessions angrily damning his father.

Too bad. But RET can't win them all. And obviously doesn't!

RET Exercise No. 8

Try to remember an event from your early life when you felt horrified, depressed, or self-hating. Then see if you can figure out your rational Beliefs (rBs) and irrational Beliefs (iBs) that you held at that time that probably led you to feeling emotionally upset. See how you hold on to them today.

Example: "My parents often made me wear ill-fitting hand-me-down clothes and I felt so ashamed that I often stayed at home and refused to play with the other kids."

Rational Beliefs (rBs): "I don't like wearing ill-fitting clothes and possibly being laughed at by the other kids. But I can bear it and still get along with the kids who may laugh at me."

Early irrational Beliefs (iBs): "I *must* not wear these ill-fitting clothes and be laughed at by the other kids. How awful and shameful. They must think I'm a fool—and they're right, I am!"

Present irrational Beliefs (iBs): "I make sure I don't wear ill-fitting clothes today. But I still think that if anyone laughs at me and thinks I'm a fool I agree that I am and feel very ashamed."

Example: "My teachers treated me uncaringly and unfairly when I was a child and that made me very angry and rebellious."

Rational Beliefs (rBs): "I wish my teachers would treat me caringly and fairly and it is most unfortunate that they don't. But that is their poor behavior and they are not totally rotten people for acting that way."

Early irrational Beliefs (iBs): "My parents *absolutely should* treat me caringly and fairly, and it is awful that they don't. They are thoroughly rotten people for acting in that horrible way and I hope they drop dead!"

Present irrational Beliefs (iBs): "Some people still treat me uncaringly and unfairly today—and they *absolutely should not*! These people are thoroughly rotten people and I hope they get severely punished!"

Whenever you think that your early experiences have made you or conditioned you to be disturbed today, recall and relive these experiences and figure out your rational Beliefs (rBs) and especially your irrational Beliefs (iBs) that mainly led to your past emotional problems, and also see how you are still clinging to these iBs today.

CHAPTER 10

Insight No. 5: Actively Dispute Your Irrational Beliefs

So you are now beginning to have insight into your irrational Beliefs—especially into your dogmatic shoulds and musts.
Great!

But you won't do yourself much good, nor will you remove your neurotic misery, unless you actively and forcefully dispute your iBs.

Understanding is not enough, any more than understanding how to drive a car will make you a good driver. What are you going to *do* about knowing the ABCs of RET and about the irrational Beliefs that you use to keep yourself disturbed?

I have twenty or more clients, at the time I write this, who are well aware of their iBs but who are doing little to dispute them. Irene has been in one of my therapy groups for four months and often helps other members by pointing out their irrationalities and vigorously showing them that there is no reason why they must be in a good relationship or have to marry. But she thinks that because she is approaching thirty-five and has never had a long-term relationship, she absolutely *must* marry very soon.

Irene keeps telling the group, "I think it would be desirable if I marry but I don't *have to.*" She then secretly sneaks in, "But I really *must*!" And she rarely challenges and rips up her own *must*—so she remains quite anxious.

Frank, another member of Irene's therapy group, shows Irene her musts, but tries to give her only practical solutions about her need to marry soon—like suggesting good places for her to meet suitable males. In his own case, he does the same thing: He only looks for "good" ways to argue with his obnoxious boss instead of giving up his own demand that his boss *must* not be obnoxious.

Josie, a third member of this group, keeps insisting that because Irene *is* getting older and because she dotes on children, she really *should* find a husband soon. Needless to say, Josie is hardly helping herself give up her own demands—that her daughter and her husband *must* be caring and fair to her—and she definitely is not helping Irene.

So RET includes *Insight No. 5: Fully acknowledge that you upset yourself with irrational musts. Acknowledging that you have musts will not in itself make them disappear. Fight them in many ways that RET provides, but above all actively challenge and dispute them.*

When you are irrational, you oppose reason (good sense) and refuse to accept reality (the way things are). Science tells you how to use reason, logic, and facts, to surrender your irrational thinking. It raises skeptical questions:

"Where is the evidence that I *must* succeed?"

"Why do people *have to* treat me fairly?"

"Where is it written that my life has *got to be* free of hassles?"

When you use scientific questioning and disputing you figure out answers like these:

"There is no evidence that I *must* succeed, though I would very much prefer to do so."

"People *don't* have to treat me fairly, although it would be lovely if they did!"

"My life never *has to be* free of major hassles and probably never will be. But I can still lead an enjoyable existence! And I can even learn and benefit from the hassles!"

Is RET a self-treatment method that specializes in arguing and persuading? It is. With a vengeance! It holds that disputing, disputing, and disputing irrational Beliefs is one of the most important means of overcoming your emotional problems.

Let us go back to the ABCs of RET and proceed to D, Disputing. How would you Dispute if you had the problem presented in Chapter 5? Let us see.

G (your Goal)—you want a good job.

A (your Activating Event)—you do badly in an interview and fail to get the job you desire.

rBs (your rational Beliefs)—"I don't like failing to get this job!

How frustrating! Too bad! How can I try to do better next time?"

iBs (your irrational Beliefs)—"No matter what, I *must* get this interviewer to like me and give me this job! If he doesn't, it's *awful*! I can't stand it! If I fail, that proves that I'm an incompetent person who will never be able to get and keep a good position."

C (Consequence of holding your irrational Beliefs)—you feel depressed and worthless. You avoid going for other interviews.

Now that we have outlined the ABCs about your Goal of getting a good job, let us proceed to D—to scientifically Dispute your irrational Beliefs (iBs):

iB—"No matter what, I *must* get this interviewer to like me and give me this job."

D (Disputing)—"Why *must* I get this interviewer to like me? Where is the evidence that he *has to* give me this job?"

E (Effective new philosophy)—"There is no reason why I *must* get this interviewer to like me, though there are several reasons why I would *prefer* that. No evidence exists that he *has to* give me this job. If the universe ruled that he *had to* give it to me, he obviously would. But it doesn't. Too bad!"

iB—"If I don't get this job, as I *must*, it's *awful*!"

D (Disputing)—"In what way is it *awful* if I don't get this job?"

E (Effective new philosophy)—"In no way. It may be damned inconvenient. But it is hardly one hundred percent inconvenient, since it could be worse. And if it were *awful* or *terrible* it would be *more than* (101 percent) inconvenient—which, of course, it can't be. So it's inconvenient! Tough!"

iB—"If I don't get this job, as I *must*, I can't stand it."

D (Disputing)—"Prove that I can't stand it."

E (Effective new philosophy)—"I can't prove that because I obviously *can* stand it. First of all, I will hardly die if I lose this job. Second, if I really couldn't *stand* it, I couldn't be happy *at all* without this job. But clearly there are many ways in which I can be happy, even if I never get as good a job as this one."

iB—"My losing this job proves that I'm an incompetent person who will never be able to get and keep a good position."

D (Disputing)—"Where is this written?"

E (Effective new philosophy)—"Only in my nutty head! If I lose this job it may not at all show that I am incompetent—but only that this particular interviewer didn't like me. And even if I acted incompetently in the interview that only indicates that I am a *person who acted badly this time* and not a totally *incompetent person.* Even if I often am incompetent at interviews, that doesn't prove that I will *never* be able to get and keep a good position. So I'd better start looking again!"

If you keep actively and vigorously Disputing your irrational Beliefs—at point D in RET—you scientifically challenge them until you prove them wrong and give them up. And you change C—in this case, your depression and self-denigration. If you keep strongly Disputing your iBs, your disturbed Consequences rarely return.

As you give up your inappropriate feelings of depression and wormhood, you are also able to change your behavior and can fairly easily keep going on more interviews and continue looking for a job.

To return to Irene, the member of my therapy group mentioned above, she finally admitted that, on the one hand, she was telling herself, "I don't *have to* marry" but, on the other hand, she was even more strongly convincing herself, "But I really *must.*" She and the other group members then kept vigorously Disputing her irrational *must* until she finally got to—and really believed—the bottom line: "It is indeed highly desirable if I marry. But if I never find a suitable mate, I can *still* be a happy person. I *can*! And will! No matter what!"

After weeks of accepting this new Effective Rational Philosophy (E), Irene's panic vanished, even though her strong desires and goals to marry remained. She was then appropriately *disappointed* but not *depressed* about still being single.

Frank, doing some amount of active Disputing but not as much as Irene, partially gave up the irrational Belief that his boss *must* not act obnoxiously, but he from time to time returned to it. Josie at first refused to surrender her demands that her daughter and her husband *must* be caring and fair to her. But when she saw how Irene overcame her panic about being single, she was able to accept, though not like, her uncaring family. As she noted to the group: "Dammit, they just *are* the way they are. And I didn't *make* them that way. They have their own fine talents at being cold and unloving. Why should they *not* behave badly—when they obviously *do!*" Believing and feeling this, Josie became less obsessed with her family and more devoted to Chinese art—which rarely treated her unjustly!

RET Exercise No. 9

Find something that you are now or have recently been emotionally upset about or that you acted foolishly about. Write it down.
  For Example:
  Someone lied to you and you felt furious and homicidal.
  You failed to do your regular exercises and you felt angry at yourself and very depressed.
  You wore an informal outfit to a formal affair and felt highly embarrassed or ashamed.
  You were severely criticized by a friend you had helped and you felt extremely hurt and self-pitying.
  You promised yourself to stop smoking and didn't stop.
  You selfishly harmed an innocent person.
  You gave into a plane phobia—drove a thousand miles to get somewhere.
  You put yourself down for not overcoming one of your phobias or compulsions.
  When you remember the present or past time that you felt disturbed or acted self-defeatingly, assume that you had an irrational should, ought, or must and look for it.
  Example: "The person who lied to me absolutely should not have done that! How terrible that she acted the way she *must* not act!"
  Also look for the common irrational Beliefs that often accompany your *musts*. Write them down:
  Awfulizing, horribleizing, terribleizing.
  Example: "Since I acted so stupidly about wearing that informal outfit to a formal affair, as I clearly *should* not have done, that's *terrible!* It's *awful* that I can't dress properly."
  "*I can't-stand-it-itis.*"
  Example: "When friends whom I have helped and supported severely criticize me, as they definitely *should* not, I *can't stand it!* I *can't bear* such ingratitude!"

Feelings of worthlessness and self-hatred.

Example: "Because I didn't follow my promise to stop smoking, as I *should* have done, I'm a *stupid, worthless person.* Considering how important it is to stop, I'm really *no good* for continuing to smoke."

Feelings of undeservingness and self-damnation.

Example: "Because I selfishly harmed my innocent friend, as I *absolutely should not* have done, I am a *damnable person* who *deserves to be punished.* I am *undeserving* of any acceptance by others and should be severely boycotted."

Belief in allness, neverness, and totality.

Example: "Now that I have stupidly given in to my plane phobia and driven a thousand miles to get from New York to Chicago, as I definitely *should not* have done, I'll *never* be able to overcome my irrational fear of planes, I'll *always* have to drive instead of fly long distances, and I am *totally* unable to conquer my phobia."

Belief in perfection, specialness, and grandiosity.

Example: "I must be perfect, special, and noble and if I am less than this, I am not really a good or worthy person. If I am not superspecial, I am nothing!"

Now actively Dispute (at point D) your irrational Beliefs (iBs) by asking scientific questions about them and assuming that if you keep questioning and challenging them you can definitely change them to preferences or give them up entirely. Here are some of the main Disputing questions you can ask:

Disputing question: "*Why is my iB true? Why does it not conform to reality?*"

Example: "Why *should not* people who lie to me do what they do—lie? Why *must* not they act in that way and why is it *terrible* if they do?"

Answer: There is no reason why they *should not* or *must* not lie, though it would be highly desirable if they didn't. Actually, if they are prone to lying right now, they *must* keep lying—for that is their nature. And if they do lie, it is hardly *terrible* (or badder than it *should* be) but only highly inconvenient. And I can live with that inconvenience."

Disputing question: "*Where is the evidence that my irrational Beliefs (iBs) are true? Where are the facts to sustain them?*"

Example: "Where is the evidence that I should not have acted stupidly and worn that informal outfit to a formal affair? Where are the facts to prove that it's *terrible* that I did so?"

Answer: "There is no evidence that I *should not* have acted so stupidly and there is considerable evidence that I am a fallible human who consequently will at times behave quite stupidly. There are no facts to prove that it's *terrible* that I did this, but only facts to show that I encouraged some people to think less of my behavior (and probably of me) and that's unfortunate, but I can still win the approval of many people and lead a good life."

Disputing question: "*Where is it written that my irrational Beliefs (iBs) are true? Who says that they exist in reality?*"

Example: "Where is it written that friends I have helped *absolutely should not* criticize me severely and that I *can't stand it* when they do? Who says that I *can't bear* such severe criticism?"

Answer: "It is only written in my head that they *must not* criticize me, since obviously they are not heeding my command. I *can* stand it when they do severely criticize me, because their words can't hurt me unless *I* sharpen them and take them too seriously. Since I won't die from their criticism and can still accept myself in spite of it, I *can* bear it—and perhaps even benefit from heeding some of it."

Disputing question: "*In what way can I support these irrational Beliefs (iBs)? How can I prove their validity?*"

Example: "In what way am I a *stupid, worthless person* because I didn't follow my promise to stop smoking, as I *should* have followed it? How does this stupid act of smoking make me *no good*?"

Answer: "In no way am *I*, a total person, *stupid and worthless* because I keep doing a stupid act like smoking. My *act* is foolish but that hardly makes me a *worthless* fool, only a *person who* is now acting foolishly, who may act less foolishly in the future, and who does many other intelligent things. *It*, this stupid act of smoking, is no good (or of little good) but *I* am not *it*. I am I, and I have the ability to do many good things and many bad acts. I also have the ability to change my bad deeds for good ones. So let me see how I can now stop smoking!"

Disputing question: "*Is there any way in which I can falsify or invalidate my irrational Beliefs (iBs)?*"

Example: "Is there any way in which I can falsify or invalidate my Belief that because I selfishly harmed my innocent friend, as I absolutely should not, I am a *damnable person* who *deserves* to be punished? Can I really prove or disprove the idea that I am undeserving of any acceptance by others and should be severely boycotted and punished?"

Answer: "No, I cannot falsify my belief that I am a *damnable person* who *deserves* to be punished. I can prove that I selfishly harmed my innocent friend, which was wrong. But I can only arbitrarily insist that the wrongness or evil makes me a *damnable, undeserving person* who absolutely *should be* punished and deprived of all human acceptance and pleasure. Concepts like damnation, undeservingness, and total unacceptability as a human imply that there is some superhuman higher power that absolutely knows when human acts are bad enough to levy such undebatable sanctions. But such superhuman powers cannot be proved or disproved, so there is no way to falsify (or to verify) these exceptionally punitive concepts. To believe in them leads to extreme self-damnation and self-deprivation. But since I cannot justify or falsify these irrational Beliefs, and they are therefore matters of pure choice, why should I choose to self-defeatingly believe them? For no good reason!"

Disputing question: "*What results will I get if I continue to hold these irrational Beliefs? What good—and harm—will it bring me to believe them?*"

Example: "What results will I get if I believe that I *absolutely should not* have given in to my plane phobia and driven a thousand miles to get from New York to Chicago, I'll *never* be able to overcome my irrational fear of planes? What results will I achieve if I firmly believe that I'll *always* have to drive instead of fly long distances?"

Answer: "Very poor results! If I rigidly hold to this overgeneralized way of thinking, I will doom myself to my all-and-never predictions and *make* my phobia a hopeless condition. Whenever I insist that I *can't* change and that I must *always* function badly, I block my progress and practically force myself to stick in the mud."

Disputing question: "*Can I choose to stop believing and following my irrational Beliefs?*"

Example: "Can I choose to believe that I do not have to be perfect, special, and noble and choose to give up the belief that if I am not all I am nothing?"

Answer: "Of course I can! Anything I choose to believe I can obviously choose not to believe. Even if I am strongly indoctrinated—or indoctrinate myself—with these nutty beliefs in my early life, I may have to make some effort to change them, but as long as they are *my* ideas I can choose to change them or give them up. Many of the things I once believed I no longer hold to, and any notion I now choose to cling to I can later change. So let me work at changing my irrational and self-defeating Beliefs to those that will bring me better results!"

Once you have written down some of your dogmatic *musts* and the other irrational Beliefs (iBs) that they tend to lead to, ask yourself the Disputing questions listed above and do your best to answer them until you at least temporarily change these Beliefs to rational preferences. Do this until you feel much better and have changed your inappropriate feelings and behaviors for more appropriate ones. Repeat this exercise whenever you feel quite disturbed or act in a distinctly self-defeating manner. If necessary, repeat it two, three, or more times a day when you feel seriously anxious, depressed, hostile, self-hating, or self-pitying.

CHAPTER 11

Insight No. 6: You Can Refuse to Upset Yourself About Upsetting Yourself

Many therapies, such as behavior therapy, try to relieve people's neurotic symptoms—their phobias, obsessions, compulsions, and addictions. Some therapies, such as existential analysis and psychoanalysis, try to go "deeper" and help clients change their philosophy, and thus prevent them from creating new symptoms in the future. RET goes still further and aims for a profound new philosophy as well as for relieving symptoms. It also helps people become unanxious and undepressed *about* their neurotic problems.[1]

RET's view that crooked thinking leads to emotional problems has much evidence to support it, as I have already noted. But it is also supported by the very nature of neurosis. As I point out in *Reason and Emotion in Psychotherapy* and *A New Guide to Rational Living*, we may drive rats and guinea pigs "neurotic" in psychological laboratories, but they do not seem to *know* they are disturbed. They don't *observe* their crazy behavior, or *think* about it, or *hate themselves* for suffering from it. Humans often do.

People continually *see* that they are anxious, *know* that worry is inefficient, *measure* how bad it is, *accept responsibility* for producing it, and *criticize* themselves for "weakly" or "stupidly" bringing it on. They then tend to make themselves anxious about their anxiety, depressed about their depression, guilty about their addictions, self-pitying about their neurosis.

George is often angry at his senile, demanding mother—and hates himself intensely for being angry at her. Cynthia smokes two packs of cigarettes a day in spite of her weak lungs and steady coughing and is very guilty about her "horrible weakness." Josef is unassertive with his womanfriend—and angry at her for "making him" afraid to assert himself.

Are disturbances about disturbances important? Indeed they are! For if George hates himself for being angry at his mother, he will tend to be so wrapped up in his self-denigration that he will have little time and energy to work on the problem of giving up his anger. If Cynthia is guilty about her "horrible weakness" of continuing to smoke when she has weak lungs, she will upset herself so severely that she may "need" more cigarettes to distract her from her self-hatred. While Josef remains angry at his woman friend for "making" him unassertive, he will be aggressive rather than assertive and will hardly work on expressing himself. By bringing on their disturbances *about* their original neuroses, George, Cynthia, and Josef will *add* considerably to their emotional problems.

This brings us to *Insight No. 6 of RET: Once you make yourself miserable about anything, you easily tend to make yourself miserable about your misery. If you look at what you are doing, you can often discover that you are making yourself anxious about your anxiety, depressed about your depression, and guilty about your rage. You really are talented at upsetting yourself!*

Don't take my word for it. Be honest with yourself. How did you really feel when you were last panicked? Yes, how did you feel *about* your panic? And *about* your last bout of depression? And *about* your severe feelings of inadequacy?

See!

The RET solution? Oddly enough, more thinking, more reasoning. When you create problems *about* problems by *observing* your bad feelings and *telling yourself* that you *must not* have these feelings, you can remove them by using Insight No. 6.

To be more precise, to stop disturbing yourself about disturbing yourself, try the following steps:

1. You *ask yourself*, "Now that I feel very anxious, am I *also* anxious *about* my anxiety?"

2. You *acknowledge*, when you find time, your secondary symptoms—such as your depression about your anxiety and your anxiety about your depression.

3. You *understand* that you have created your secondary

symptoms—yes, *made* yourself panicked about your panic, self-hating about your self-hatred.

4. You *recognize* that because *you* brought on your secondary feelings of misery, *you* also have the ability to work at changing them.

What next?

Suppose that, using RET, you have made yourself fully aware that you feel, let us say, anxiety about your anxiety—or panic about your panic! What do you do now?

You next take these Disputing steps:

1. You *assume* that you created your panic about your panic with some absolutistic musts—such as, "I *must* not be panicked! I *have to* be calm!"

2. You *seek out, probe for* your *musts* until you find them: "Oh, yes. I now see that I *do* believe that I *must* never be panicked, or else I'll end up in the loony bin. And that would *really* be *terrible!*"

3. You actively Dispute your musts until you come up with—and truly believe!—Effective Rational Philosophies. Like this:

iB (irrational Beliefs)—"It's *awful* to be panicked!"

D (Disputing)—"Where is the evidence that it's *awful*?"

E (Effective Rational Philosophy)—"Nowhere except in my foolish thinking! It's *only* very inconvenient, but I can always stand it—and work to get rid of my panic about panic."

iB—"I *must* not be panicked!"

D—"Where is that law of the universe written?"

E—"Nowhere. Only in the heads of crooked-thinking humans like me! If the universe ruled that I must not be panicked, I couldn't possibly be. Obviously its rule is that I *can be* extremely anxious—if I allow myself to be!"

iB—"If I am panicked, I'll end up in the loony bin and that would *really* be terrible!"

D—"Is this true?"

E—"Nonsense! I and billions of other people have been panicked before and have somehow managed to stay out of the mental hospital. Feelings of panic are painful but rarely produce nervous breakdowns. Otherwise, all of us humans would be confined! And even if the worst comes to the worst—which is most unlikely—and I do for a while get hospitalized, that would be highly uncomfortable. But I can still survive, calm down, and lead a happy life. If I *think* I can!"

If you Dispute (D) your irrational Beliefs (iBs) leading to your emotional Consequence (C) of anxiety *about* anxiety, you can then keep *thinking and planning* to rid yourself of it and to see that you rarely bring it back. Your final conclusions will tend to be:

1. "I am never an *incompetent or rotten person* for making myself anxious and making myself anxious about my anxiety. I am merely a *person who* has some rotten philosophies—which I can work at changing."

2. "No matter how badly I inconvenience and handicap myself with feelings of stress and panic, they are *only* that: *inconvenient.* Never *awful* or *horrible*! Never *unbearable*! Only a royal pain in the neck!"

Once you keep making these conclusions, you can go back to your original feelings of panic (such as your horror about being rejected by someone), discover your irrational Beliefs that are creating the panic (for example, "I cannot be alone and be happy!"); and Dispute these iBs and remove your original anxiety.

Insight No. 6 of RET, as you can see, indicates that you easily create primary emotional problems and secondary problems *about* your original ones. It encourages you to give up, first, your secondary neurosis—and then to undo your primary one.

Insight No. 6 also shows you how you can create third-level disturbances and how to work against them, too. Gerald, for example, first made himself anxious about doing well at work (primary problem). Then he became addicted to alcohol in order to temporarily calm his anxiety (secondary problem). Then he damned himself severely for his drinking (third level problem). Because of his third-level self-blame he upset himself so much that he did worse at work and (to soothe his anxiety) drank much more.

If you heed *Insight No. 6*, you will undo your second-level and third-level emotional problems, then get back to working against your primary disturbances, and thus comprehensively help yourself.

Here are some follow-ups on the clients mentioned previously in this chapter:

George examined his irrational Belief, "I *must* never be angry at my mother, even though she neglected me as a child and now demands that I devote myself to her in her old age. What a louse I am!" He first accepted *himself* with his anger—then, free of his self-hatred, he stopped demanding that his mother be nondemanding, and gave up hatred of her (though not his dislike for her behavior).

Cynthia, after much rethinking, was able to strongly repeat to herself many times, "My continuing to smoke is indeed a bad weakness. But beating myself for smoking only makes me weaker! If *I* am no good for smoking, how can rotten *me* ever do a good thing like stopping? Never! So even if I keep foolishly smoking, I am determined to stop my self-beating!" As soon as she ceased her self-blaming, Cynthia found it much easier to stay at five cigarettes a day, instead of her usual two packs.

Josef acknowledged that his woman friend really was making it difficult—though not impossible—for him to assert himself. But by showing himself that she had a right, as a human, to be wrong, he lost his anger at her—and then, despite his fear and discomfort, he was able to force himself to be more and more assertive, until acting that way became natural and easy.

Gerald, with the help of one of my regular therapy groups, first worked at his third-level problem—his downing himself for his alcoholism—by showing himself that his drinking was stupid but that *he* was not a stupid, hopeless person. Then he tackled his secondary symptom (low frustration tolerance) which accompanied his irrational Belief, "I can't stand feeling anxious, so I must immediately relieve myself by drinking!" Finally, he went back to his primary symptom, his anxiety created by his demand that he *had to* do very well at work—and he was able to make himself *concerned* but no longer *over*concerned about his job performances, and to become much less anxious. On all three levels he improved—and his drinking and his work considerably improved, too. As his anxiety, low frustration tolerance, and self-damning decreased, he was able to stop drinking altogether and lead a much more productive life.

RET Exercise No. 10

This is an exercise in self-honesty. Dishonesty with yourself is usually the result of your self-downing. You feel ashamed to admit the truth—as when you fail miserably at something or see that others are laughing at you—so you lie to yourself and deny your errors and your foolishness.

What you can do now is to honestly admit when you recently felt upset—felt anxious, depressed, or enraged. Examples.

Were you anxious about your children or other close relatives coming home later than expected?

Were you panicked about a pain in your chest, thinking it might be a heart attack?

Were you depressed about the death of a relative or close friend?

Were you enraged about terrorism directed against innocent civilians?

These are anxieties about real major or important events and you probably were able to accept your reactions and deal with them. But how about some recent minor or unimportant events? For Example:

Suppose you notice you have a spot on your shirt and are anxious about the strangers on the bus or subway who might notice it?

Or suppose you are at a party or a convention and forgot someone's name and are panicked lest that person see that you have forgotten it?

Or suppose you were unassertive with your barber and are afraid that people will discover that you let him cut your hair too short?

Or suppose you have to go to the bathroom in the midst of a concert and are ashamed that people will think you foolish and disruptive for going?

Look for minor incidents like these and acknowledge that you were really anxious, panicked, or ashamed about them—and that you were anxious about your anxiety, ashamed of your shame, depressed about your panic. Can you be quite honest with yourself? Can you fully admit your original panic about this slight failing or screw-up—and can you admit your secondary panic of letting people know about your original anxiety? Force yourself to be honest If it kills you!

Now do something more:

1. Laugh to yourself about your panic and your panic about your panic. See how ridiculous it is that you absolutely *need* people's approval for almost everything you do—and that you need their approval for your needing their approval! See how funny this is!

2. As a shame-attacking exercise, tell someone—better, tell *several* people—about your "shameful" feelings. Let them know what a trivial thing you upset yourself about. Show them how you made yourself upset about your upsetness. Be ruthlessly open and honest to others about how afraid you are—and how fearful of your fearfulness!

3. Find your main *musts* about your original feelings of panic. For example. "I *must* remember this person's name! I *must* not have to ask him, once again, what his name is! I *must* not insult him by forgetting who he is! I *must* not let him know I stupidly forgot!"

4. Find your *musts* about your secondary anxiety. For example: "I *must* not show my anxiety to others! I *must* not be so anxious over trifles! I *must* get over my anxiety immediately!"

5. Rip up these musts and change them to preferences.

6. Continue to observe and admit that you often make yourself anxious or panicked over many little things. Continue to accept yourself with your anxiety, to often confess it to others, and to find and dispute the musts with which you create it

CHAPTER 12

Insight No. 7: Solving Reality Problems as Well as Emotional Problems

Although RET is often accused of being a superficial form of therapy—because its ABCs are simple and easy for almost anyone to understand—it actually is more comprehensive than most other therapies. For it sees everyone—including you—as affecting and being affected by the people and the environment around them.

You live in a social system—with your family, friends, business associates, acquaintances, and strangers. You, to some degree, affect these others; and they affect and influence you.

You also live in an external environment—with air, vegetation, roads, buildings, weather conditions, machines, autos, etc. All of these, too, affect you; and you, in turn, act on them.

Finally, you live in your own body—with bones, blood, internal organs, skin, nerves, and other tissues that strongly influence you. Again, your doings—such as eating, drinking, exercising, thinking, and feeling—importantly affect your body.

Living in this complicated environment, you have (as noted previously in this book) basic Goals (G) which you bring to the Activating Events of your life. These Goals create many practical problems for you to try to solve. Such as:

How shall I get a good education?

What shall I do to find a suitable mate?

Which profession shall I choose and how shall I succeed at it?

What recreations do I find enjoyable and worthy of my time and effort?

Once you recognize these reality problems, you can try to solve them—or you can foolishly choose to make yourself upset about them. If you upset yourself, you then have a problem about a problem—an emotional problem (or neurosis) about your reality problem (how to survive and enjoy yourself).

RET is more systematic than most other therapies in that it encourages you to tackle both your original practical difficulties and your later emotional difficulties—though not necessarily in that order. In fact, it often encourages you, when you have a neurotic problem, to first work at solving that dilemma—and then to tackle your practical problems.

Why so? For several reasons:

1. While you are anxious or depressed about making a decision—such as, "Shall I stay with my love partner or end our relationship?"—you may be unable to see which of your desires (to stay or leave) is greater. Your guilt about leaving, for example, may prevent you from seeing that you really want to go. Or your anger at your partner may push aside your real desire to stay.

2. You may spend so much time and energy being disturbed that you have little left to devote to solving your practical problem. Thus, you may spend so much time whining about having to decide whether to leave your love partner that you never get around to actually making a clear decision.

3. You may be so upset about having a practical problem and knowing no good and quick solution to it that you may not be able to keep your thoughts in order to help solve it.

RET, therefore, encourages you first to solve your emotional upsetness (your problem about a problem) and then carefully consider your practical decisions.

This brings us to RET's *Insight No. 7: As you attempt to solve your practical life problems, look carefully to discover whether you have any emotional problems—such as feelings of anxiety or depression—about these practical issues. If so, seek out and actively Dispute your dogmatic, musturbatory thinking that leads to your emotional difficulties. While working to reduce your neurotic feelings, go back to your practical difficulties and use effective self-management and problem-solving methods to tackle them.*

Joani greatly wanted to finish college but had little money and had to commute fifty miles to do so. Rough going! But she made it much rougher by telling herself, "I *must* finish college and do so soon! This means that I have to work hard at my job and at school, and also spend time commuting—and that's unfair and things *shouldn't* be that unfair! Besides, my father keeps telling me that I haven't the ability to finish—and maybe he's right. If so, that would be *awful* and I'd *never* get any of the good things I really want in life! I hate my rotten father for doing this to me!"

With these strong irrational Beliefs, Joani took her original practical problems and used them to make herself feel anxious, depressed, angry, and self-hating. Naturally, her disturbed feelings greatly interfered with her solving her practical (money, school, work, and commuting) problems—not to mention her trouble communicating with her father.

Joani and I first worked at revealing and changing her dogmatic musts about herself, about her father, and about the school situation. Then, as we did this, I helped her improve her practical problem skills and figure out alternate solutions that her upsetness blocked her from discovering—including borrowing money and living and working closer to her college. I also helped her to learn communication skills (to get along better with her father) and to acquire organizing and study skills (and thus be capable of doing more schoolwork in less time).

You, too, can first change your irrational Beliefs and the disturbed emotional Consequences to which they lead. You can then go back to A (the Activating Events of your life) and use the problem-solving and other skills to make your decisions more practical and pleasurable.

To improve your life, you can use RET to acquire assertiveness training, time management methods, relationship skills, sex education, job advancement methods, and various other skills that may help you lead a more self-fulfilling existence. Because RET deals with thinking *and* behavior and because it includes corrective teaching, it is a pioneering problem-solving and skill-training approach to therapy.[1]

Which once again shows that it is comprehensive! It is a "systems theory" of human behavior that is truly systematic! By helping you to understand your disruptive feelings (C) about your life events (A), and to change your ideas (B) that produce these feelings, it enables you to work at reorganizing your As, Bs, and Cs. And to see and rearrange the complicated ways in which A, B, and C interact.

RET Exercise No. 11

Think of a practical problem that you want to solve or a decision
you want to make. For example, consider:

> How to get a better job.
> How to give a good speech.
> How to win a golf game.
> How to write a term paper.
> How to drive to a strange city.
> How to relate well to others.
> How to have more enjoyable sex.

Think about these decisions:

> Which TV set to buy.
> Which house to purchase.
> Which person to choose as a partner in a game.
> Which courses to take at school.
> Which suit or dress to wear to a party.
> Which life career to choose.
> Which exercise program to select.

Look for any emotional or behavioral problems that you have
about these practical problems. For example:

> Are you anxious about getting a good job and keeping it?
> Would you be ashamed if you gave a poor speech?
> Would you be depressed if you played golf poorly?
> Are you continuing to procrastinate about writing a term paper?
> Are you angry about driving in a strange city?
> Are you afraid to try to relate to others?
> Do you blame yourself severely for having sex problems?
> Do you compulsively keep getting more and more information
>   about TV sets before you decide to buy one?
> Are you extremely fearful that the house you purchase will col-
>   lapse or be burned down?
> Do you mercilessly blame yourself for picking the wrong partner
>   in a game?

Do you keep changing your school courses even after the term
  has begun?

Do you agonize over choosing a suit or dress to wear to a party?

Do you do nothing about choosing a career?

Do you try one exercise program after another and quit before it
  really gets under way?

If you are anxious, ashamed, depressed, or enraged about your
practical problems or if you are indecisive, phobic, or compulsive
about making decisions, look for your dogmatic demands—for your
shoulds, oughts, and musts, and for your awfulizing, self-downing,
and I-can't-stand-it-itis that accompany them. For example:

"I *must* get a good job and *have to* keep it when I do!"

"My speech *must* come off marvelously! It would be shameful if
they laugh at me when I give it!"

"I *should* have played that golf game better! What a hopelessly
rotten athlete I am!"

"Writing that damned term paper *ought to be* easier! I *can't
stand* the hassle of doing it! I'll do it later!"

"These blasted city streets *should be* laid out better, with much
clearer signs! How *awful* that they are giving me needless trouble!"

"I *must* get the very best TV set for the money! I *can't bear it* if I
get gypped!"

"Suppose something dreadful happens to a house after I purchase it! I *must have a guarantee* that everything will be all right
with it!"

"I'll never forgive myself if I pick the wrong partner for this
game. What a complete idiot I would be!"

"I *must* have the best course and the best teacher. It would be
horrible if I wasted my time in this course. If I don't change it right
away, even though it's against the school rules, I'm a perfect
wimp!"

"If I choose the wrong suit or dress for this party and people
laugh at me for picking it, I might as well kill myself!"

"Every possible career I choose has too many hassles that go
with it. I *can't* bear any career with so many hassles!"

"I *shouldn't* have to keep exercising but should be perfectly
healthy without doing it!"

Actively dispute your shoulds and musts, your awfulizing, your can't-stand-it-itis, and your self-downing. For example:

Disputing: "Why *must* I get a good job and where is it written that I *have to* keep it when I do?" *Answer*: "I don't *have to* get or keep a good job, but very much *want* to. So I'll keep pushing to get one."

Disputing: "Where is it written that my speech *must* come off marvelously? How would it be shameful if they laugh at me when I give it?" *Answer*: "It is not written anywhere—except in the foolish scripts I write for myself! It would be unfortunate if they laughed at me when I gave it, but only my speech would be bad and I would not be a *bad, incompetent, shameful person.*

Disputing: "Why *should* I have played that golf game better? How does playing it badly make me a hopelessly rotten athlete?" *Answer*: "No reason why I *should* or *must* play it better, but it would be great if I did! It only shows that I was rotten at playing golf this time and not that I *never* would be good at playing it or at any other sport!"

Disputing: "Prove that doing the term paper *ought to be* easier. In what way can't I *stand* the hassle of doing it?" *Answer*: "Doing the paper *ought to be* just as bad as it is. For that's the way it is right now. I don't like the hassle of doing it but I'll like even less the hassles that stem from *not* doing it. So back to the drawing board!"

Disputing: "Show why the blasted city streets *should be* laid out better, with much clearer signs. Is it really *awful* that it's giving me this much trouble?" *Answer*: "I can only show that it would be lovely if the city streets were laid out better and had much clearer signs. But I cannot show that this is *necessary*, because if it were these streets *would* be laid out to suit me. Obviously, the city planners do not care the way I want them to care. Tough! But I can still find my way around!"

Disputing: "*Must* I really get the best TV set for the money? *Can't* I bear it if I get gypped?" *Answer*: "No, I clearly don't *have to* get the best set for the money. I *can* end up with an inferior one. And if I actually get gypped and end up with an inferior set, I can *still* get a lot of pleasure out of it. That would be too bad—but it would still be more good than bad. And if I don't take the risk and buy one of the sets available, I'll never enjoy TV at all! So I'd better choose one!"

Disputing: "Do I really *need* a guarantee that everything will be all right with any house that I purchase? Will the world come to an end if something dreadful happens to it?" *Answer*: "No, it would be great if I had such a guarantee—but guarantees like that simply don't exist. All I can get is a high degree of probability that any house I purchase will last a long time in spite of all the things that could happen to it. And even if the house somehow gets demolished, my life will go on and I can still enjoy it."

Disputing: "Can I forgive myself if I pick the wrong partner for this game and consequently we lose the match? Would picking the wrong partner make me an idiot?" *Answer*: "Of course I can forgive myself for making a poor choice of a partner. That would be a foolish act but it would hardly make me a totally stupid person. Since I am fallible, I will often make foolish choices, but I will not *always* make them or be *damnable* for making them. I can decide to accept myself, if not my poor decisions, and thereby prepare myself to learn and make better decisions in the future."

Disputing: "Do I *really* have to take the best course and have the best teacher? Does it *truly* make me a wimp if I don't rebel against the school rules and make them change my courses?" *Answer*: "No, it is obviously unnecessary for me to take the best course and to have the best teacher, though that would be highly desirable. If I go along with the school rules and don't make them change my course I won't be acting wimpishly but merely will be following normal restrictions. And even if I do act weakly, that never makes me a *total wimp* or a *weak person*."

Disputing: "Why does every possible career I choose have too many hassles that go with it? Where is the evidence that I can't bear any career with so many hassles?" *Answer*: "Just about any career I choose will have *many* hassles but not *too* many. Because it is the nature of careers to have hassles—they all do! Too bad— but unless I accept such hassles I'll end up with *no* career—and thus have *worse* problems! I may never *like* the difficulties of a career I choose, but I definitely can *stand* them. And I'd damned well better do so—if I want any career at all!"

Once you find your irrational Beliefs (iBs) that interfere with your solving your practical problem and from making good decisions, then go back to these original problems and do your best to solve them. Some problem-solving skills you can use are these:

> State a problem as clearly as you can. For example:
> What shall I do to get a good job?
> What step had I better take first?
> What steps shall I take next?
> Who should I consult about getting a good job?
> Can any of my friends possibly help me?
> What kind of a resume—or several resumes—shall I write?
> How can I get help with my resumes?
> Shall I let my past employers know I am looking, to be fully sure
>   they give me good references?
> What shall I do to have better job interviews?
> Et cetera.

Write down a good many problem-solving questions, such as these, on any practical problems you wish to solve. Then outline— and preferably put on paper—your answers. Then make a plan to act on and to implement these ideas. Then follow this plan—yes, *push yourself* to follow this plan.

If everything goes well, fine. Continue to solve your practical problems and issues. If you don't follow your plan, or follow it poorly, or get upset about the results of following it, assume that you have some emotional difficulties about your practical difficulties—and go back to the ABCs of RET, again, to see what they are and how you can deal with them. As you keep resolving your emotional problems, go back, once again, to your practical questions to work out, as above, solutions for them. Keep shuttling back and forth from your practical to your emotional and once again your practical problems. And don't expect any perfect or super-marvelous solutions. For that silly expectation will only enhance your emotional dilemmas and make everything much worse!

RET Exercise No. 12

You cannot very well solve practical problems or make good decisions without taking some risks. Typical risks are:

Taking too long to solve a problem or make a decision.

Spending too much time and energy to solve it or decide on a
   solution.
Taking too little time and trouble to plan and decide what to do.
Picking the wrong decision and having to live with it.
Doing well with your practical problems at first and later failing
   at them.
Finding a fairly good solution but not a great one which you
   would really like to find.

If you tend to be overconcerned about solving a problem or making a decision and to take too much time and energy with it, free
yourself to take the risk of planning and deciding on it more
quickly. Thus, give yourself a limited amount of time to make up
your job resume, to get a list of people to send it to, to send out
letters to these people, and to start going on job interviews. Don't
prepare too much. Take the chance that you may do poorly. Show
yourself that you can learn by your errors and probably do better
next time.

If, when you force yourself to plan and decide on some important tasks quickly, you refuse to do so or you achieve this goal and
upset yourself because your plans and decisions are not good
enough, fill out a RET Self-Help Form about your emotional problem. Such as the following pages.

RET SELF-HELP FORM

Institute for Rational-Emotive Therapy
45 East 65th Street, New York, N.Y. 10021
(212) 535-0822

(A) ACTIVATING EVENTS, thoughts, or feelings that happened just before I felt emotionally disturbed or acted self-defeatingly: _Made decision about taking a job fairly quickly_

(C) CONSEQUENCE or CONDITION—disturbed feeling or self-defeating behavior—that I produced and would like to change: _Great anxiety_

(B) BELIEFS—Irrational BELIEFS (IBs) leading to my CONSEQUENCE (emotional disturbance or self-defeating behavior). Circle all that apply to these ACTIVATING EVENTS (A).	**(D) DISPUTES** for each circled IRRATIONAL BELIEF. Examples: *"Why MUST I do very well?"* *"Where is it written that I am a BAD PERSON?"* *"Where is the evidence that I MUST be approved or accepted?"*	**(E) EFFECTIVE RATIONAL BELIEFS (RBs)** to replace my IRRATIONAL BELIEFS (IBs). *Examples: "I'd PREFER to do very well but I don't HAVE TO." "I am a PERSON WHO acted badly, not a BAD PERSON." "There is no evidence that I HAVE TO be approved, though I would LIKE to be."*
1. (I MUST do well or very well!)	_Why must I?_	_No reason — though I'd rather make decisions well!_
2. I am a BAD OR WORTHLESS PERSON when I act weakly or stupidly.		

3. I MUST be approved or accepted by people I find important!

4. I am a BAD, UNLOVABLE PERSON if I get rejected.

5. People MUST treat me fairly and give me what I NEED!

6. People who act immorally are undeserving, ROTTEN PEOPLE!

7. People MUST live up to my expectations or it is TERRIBLE!

8. My life MUST have few major hassles or troubles.

Does it really have To have few hassles?

No, that would be lovely! But it can easily have ill the hassles it really does have.

9. I CAN'T STAND really bad things or very difficult people!

(OVER)

Irrational Belief	Disputing Question	Rational Response
10. It's AWFUL or HORRIBLE when major things don't go my way!	How is it horrible?	In No way! It's only a pain in the ass.
11. I CAN'T STAND IT when life is really unfair!		
12. I NEED to be loved by someone who matters to me a lot!		
13. I NEED a good deal of immediate gratification and HAVE TO feel miserable when I don't get it!	Do I need it?	Never. I only strongly want it.

Additional Irrational Beliefs:

14. I should be able to make quick decisions & still always make them well.	Where is this indicated?	Only in my crazy head. I'd better make quick decisions & take the risk of screwing them up.
15		

16. This job I took must turn out well.

Really?? Must it? Of course not. If it turns out poorly, too bad! I'll just get another one.

17

18

(F) FEELINGS and BEHAVIORS I experienced after arriving at my EFFECTIVE RATIONAL BELIEFS: Concern but not horror about this quick decision

I WILL WORK HARD TO REPEAT MY EFFECTIVE RATIONAL BELIEFS FORCEFULLY TO MYSELF ON MANY OCCASIONS SO THAT I CAN MAKE MYSELF LESS DISTURBED NOW AND ACT LESS SELF-DEFEATINGLY IN THE FUTURE.

Joyce Sichel, Ph.D. and Albert Ellis, Ph.D.

CHAPTER 13

Insight No. 8: Changing Thoughts by Acting Against Them

As I noted in the previous chapter, you are influenced by your social groups, your environment, and your own body. But, if you would really understand yourself and your emotional problems, you had better also see that your thoughts, feelings, and behaviors all affect each other.

In my first major paper on RET, which I presented in 1956 and published in the *Journal of General Psychology*, I stated that humans rarely, if ever, have *pure* thoughts, emotions, or behaviors. Feelings *include* thoughts and actions, and they are also followed by thoughts *about* your emotions.

Particularly when you have steady feelings—as when you hate someone for years—you prolong and keep reviving these feelings by thinking, imagining, and rating what you and others do.[1]

Roberto was beaten by his father when he was fifteen and insisted that the pain of the beating and the fact that it was done in front of one of his friends clearly *caused* him to feel enraged at his father and humiliated before his friend. But Roberto was wrong—because some boys, under the same conditions, would have felt anxious instead of enraged and defiant rather than ashamed. So Roberto very likely *created* his rage and shame by thinking, within a few seconds of being beaten by his father:

1. "That bastard *shouldn't* beat me like this, especially when I haven't done anything wrong!"

2. "My friend must think I am a weakling for letting my father beat me. I *shouldn't* be so weak! How shameful it is for me to let father get away with this unfair beating!"

Roberto didn't remember, when I saw him fourteen years later, thinking anything like this—and sometimes insisted that he *automatically*, without any thinking on his part, became angry and ashamed because of his father's unfair beating in front of his friend. I showed him that we rarely feel without thinking, and he partially accepted this.

He was much more convinced when I showed him that he had kept alive his feelings with hate-creating thoughts like: "How *could* my father have been so cruel and unjust to me when I was in no position to fight him back? He *shouldn't* have done an awful thing like that! That bastard!" And, every time he contacted his parent, he *continued* to upset himself with thoughts like, "Even though I was much smaller and weaker than he at that time, I *should* have done my best to bite him, kick him in the balls, or do something to stop him! How shameful that I didn't!"

Moral: pure feelings rarely, if ever, exist. And even if they do—if you see an object flying at you and you immediately, without a thought, feel panicked—your feelings last for a few seconds and do not develop into real disturbances. Unless you *then* have irrational Beliefs *about* them. Such as: "Hell! That object almost killed me—as it *must* not do!" Or: "I *shouldn't* be panicked! How foolish of me to panic like this!"

So whenever you feel emotionally upset, look for your musturbatory thinking that is at the bottom of your upsetness—track down your silly demands and strive to change them.

But, says RET, just as your thoughts create feelings and behaviors, the latter also affect your thinking. When Roberto raged at his father, he could hardly think straight and he "unthinkingly" did foolish things—such as stubbornly refusing to lend his father rent money and thereby harming his mother, whom he loved.

So thoughts, feelings, and behaviors interact with and circularly affect each other. Crazy ideas create frantic feelings and strange acts. Hysterical feelings bring on foolish notions and behaviors. Rash actions produce nutty convictions and insane deeds. Thoughts, moreover, lead to other thoughts, feelings to new feelings, actions to different actions. The influence of thoughts, emotions, and activities on each other never seems to stop!

Suppose you want to change your obsessions, compulsions, phobias, and addictions. What then? Well, no one method will work for you all of the time. Sometimes using one philosophy to rid yourself of your anxiety will work—and sometimes it won't. Often, fully expressing your feelings will considerably help you—and often deliberately avoiding your feelings, and instead distracting yourself with some intellectual pursuit, will serve you better. At times, you will best ward off disturbances by trying every therapeutic method you can think of—the long and the short and the tall!

Give up any prejudices about which technique *should* or *must* work. Freely experiment! Try almost any treatment plan that seems sound for a reasonable length of time. But don't necessarily stick with it forever. You are not *any* seeker after help, or an *average* troubled person. You are *you*—and what goes for, or against, you is not the same as what is good or bad for anyone else. Remember *that* as you go about your self-therapy experiments.

So there practically never is one and only one helpful way. According to RET, you can often find one *main*, most *elegant* path to undo your neurotic difficulties. That is, make a profound change in your thinking that will curtail your upsetness, keep it from coming back, and prevent you from manufacturing new emotional problems in the future.

Fine: let us for the moment grant this. Even then, there is no *one* way for you to produce this new dramatic outlook. Many roads lead to Rome!

As I pointed out in 1962 in *Reason and Emotion in Psychotherapy*, and as Joseph Wolpe, Hans Eysenck, Isaac Marks, Albert Bandura, Stanley Rachman, and other behavior therapists later asserted, sometimes the best—or indeed the only—way to change a fixed idea is to force yourself to *act* against it: to engage in *live* homework assignments. This kind of forced—yes, *forced*—activity may show you that you *can* surrender an obsessive, compulsive, or frightful belief.[1] Similarly, if you work directly on your feelings, and vividly experience and express them, you may more thoroughly change your crooked thoughts than by directly disputing these irrational Beliefs.[2]

Let us, then, state *Insight No. 8: You can change irrational Beliefs (iBs) by acting against them: by performing behaviors that contradict them.*

In fact, it is doubtful if you ever truly change an irrational Belief until you literally act (and act *many times*) against it. Similarly, you practically never permanently stop your compulsive behaviors until you *think* about changing them and *decide* to do so—again and again!

Some psychologists have spread the tale that RET was at first purely intellectual and that it only later added behavioral methods. Fiction! I was a cognitive-behavioral sex therapist in 1943 when I first started to do psychotherapy and I wrote pioneering papers on active-directive sex therapy in the 1940s and 1950s, and summarized some of this material in my 1954 book, *The American Sexual Tragedy*—which was denounced by many passive Freudian and Rogerian therapists.[3] Although I largely abandoned behavioral methods when I practiced psychoanalysis between 1949 and 1953, I found psychoanalysis incredibly inefficient and therefore went back to cognitive-behavioral methods in 1953, as I was beginning to create RET.

My strong bias in favor of behavior therapy stemmed from my successful experiments with myself when I was nineteen years old and had no idea of becoming a therapist. I often tell the story of how, being unusually shy of speaking in public, I forced myself, for three months, to give many political talks.

I told myself, following several philosophers, that nothing terrible would happen to me if I spoke badly. I followed the teachings of the pioneer behavior therapist, John B. Watson, who showed that *active* reconditioning, or forcing yourself to keep doing what you are afraid of doing, really rids you of irrational fears.[4] So I expected—intellectually!—to overcome my fear of public speaking. And I did.

However—surprise, surprise!—I unexpectedly began to *enjoy* speaking in public, and have had fun doing it for over fifty years. To my astonishment, I made a hundred and eighty degree turnabout of my extreme fear.

Seeing that forcing myself to do uncomfortable things worked, I decided to do the same with my enormous fear of meeting new women. Because of my terrible fear of rejection, I never—and I mean *never*—approached strange women, although I went to walk and read in the Bronx Botanical Gardens about 250 days a year and saw a number of desirable women with whom I was eager to talk and date, and who also seemed to be flirting with me.

So I gave myself the activity homework assignment of talking to every young woman I found sitting alone on one of the park benches. No exceptions! No cop-outs!

Although very fearful and uncomfortable, I forced myself to carry out this assignment—made myself open a conversation with over one hundred women in a single month. Yes, one hundred "stranger" encounters—the kind I had always wanted to make but had fearfully avoided up to that time.

I received no direct reward from these pick-ups—since only one of these one hundred females made a date with me and she never showed up!—but I completely overcame my fear of encountering strange women, and have easily been able to talk to them for the rest of my life. For by getting rejected so many times, I *saw* that nothing dreadful happened—no name-calling, no vomiting and running away and screaming, no calling a cop! And I *concluded* that I *could* talk to strange women, fail to date them, and *still* lead a highly enjoyable existence.

I also saw that behavioral methods—particularly *acting* against one's fears—often work better to change irrational Beliefs than do purely intellectual methods. And when I later found that psycholoanalysis helped my clients very little and that talking them out of their irrational Beliefs (iBs) helped much more, I also realized that there are *many* ways of changing human attitudes—and that actively doing-what-you-are-scared-witless-of-doing is one of the best.

So, from its start, RET has always included a variety of thinking, affective, and action methods. Over the years, it has added many therapy techniques, but it was decidedly multimodal (to use Arnold Lazarus's term) from the start.[5]

Ironically, although the outstanding behavior therapist, Joseph Wolpe, has consistently opposed "cognitive" therapy, his famous systematic desensitization technique uses imagination, teaching, and other forms of thinking. RET, however, prefers more risk-taking activity homework assignments and is therefore *more* behavioral than many popular behavior therapies.

In the case of Roberto, noted at the beginning of this chapter, he agreed to often do the homework of Disputing his irrational Beliefs that his father absolutely *should not* have beaten him when he was a child and that he positively *ought not* have been a "weakling" who let his father get away with these beatings. I also helped him devise and carry out two activity homework assignments: (1) Keep talking to his father regularly instead of (as he had been doing) completely avoiding him. (2) Stand up to him in a firm but unhostile manner instead of backing down or screaming at him (as he had usually done before).

As a result of this combined thinking and behavioral RET approach, Roberto gave up his rage toward his father and himself within a period of seven weeks. He continues to work on being tolerant and self-accepting several years after his therapy sessions ended.

RET Exercise No. 13

Think of something you are irrationally afraid of doing, such as:

Speaking poorly in public.
Writing an inadequate essay or report.
Drawing badly.
Being rejected by someone you care for.
Riding in a fast elevator.
Breaking into an ongoing conversation.
Dancing in public.
Talking to strangers.
Taking a difficult course.
Being laughed at by others.
Playing a game or sport badly.

Force yourself to do one of the things that you most fear and try to do it many times in rapid succession. Once you decide to do it, don't hesitate, or cop out. Do it and do it and do it!

While you are doing this "fearful" thing, show yourself that it is not really dangerous or fearful. Show yourself that:

You will hardly die of doing it.
You will be in no real physical danger.
You may come to enjoy it.
You can learn by doing it.
You will add to your life by conquering your irrational fear.
You will have the great challenge of overcoming it.
You will eliminate the endless restrictions and frustrations of
    indulging in your fear.

You will be working at disciplining yourself and overcoming your low frustration tolerance.

You will save time and energy by giving up your obsession with it.

You will behave more efficiently as you overcome this fear.

You will gain more approval from others.

You will help ward off physical and psychosomatic ailments, such as ulcers and high blood pressure.

You will greatly reduce your negative feelings of anxiety, depression, self-downing, and self-pity.

You will find life on the whole much more enjoyable.

RET Exercise No. 13A

You may not see that you irrationally fear or are anxious about certain acts but see yourself, instead, as being ashamed, embarrassed, or humiliated to perform them. Thus, you may not see yourself as being "afraid" to wear an unstylish dress or jacket or of telling someone about one of your weaknesses, but you may never do these things because you feel they are "shameful," "embarrassing," or "humiliating."

RET considers feelings of shame or humiliation illegitimate because they almost always include a rational element—"I did something people consider wrong or stupid, and I would not like them to disapprove of me for doing it"—and they also include an irrational or self-downing element—"Therefore, I am a rotten or stupid person."

To combat this second, irrational element of shame, I created, in the late 1960s, my famous shame-attacking exercise—which is designed to help people stop feeling irrationally ashamed of anything, even when they perform and are disapproved of for some silly, stupid, incompetent, weak, or foolish act.

To help you act against your irrational Beliefs and disturbed feelings, you can benefit from doing some shame-attacking exercises. To do so, you select something that you personally feel is shameful or embarrassing to do in public. For example:

Dress inappropriately.

Say something foolish to a group of people.

Confess some weakness that people usually despise, such as, "I can't spell well."

Act strangely, such as singing in the street or holding up a black umbrella on a sunny day.

Yell out the stops on a train or bus.

Tell someone that something is radically wrong with you, such as, "I just got out of the mental hospital. What month is this?"

Say something that is unusually sexy, such as saying to a male or female companion in a loud voice so that others can hear, "Wasn't it great that we had sex five times last night?"

Refuse to tip a waiter or cabdriver who has given you poor service.

Return food to the kitchen of a restaurant when it is badly done.

Walk a banana on a leash, as if it is a pet dog.

Try to get a watch fixed in a shoe-repair shop.

Ask people for a left-handed monkey wrench.

When you do this act that you consider silly or shameful, make sure that, first, you do not get into any real trouble. Don't for example, expose yourself publicly and risk getting arrested; and don't tell your boss he or she is a worm and risk getting fired.

Second, don't do anything that would harm someone else, such as slap someone in the face or keep bothering someone.

The main things to keep in mind, as you do this shame-attacking exercise, is to work on yourself while doing it so that you do *not* feel ashamed or humiliated even when others clearly disapprove of you. You can stubbornly *refuse* to feel ashamed by telling yourself such self-statements as these:

"So people think I am stupid or foolish. Too bad! Let them think so!"

"Actually, by doing this 'shameful' act I am helping myself overcome my self-downing. And that is great!"

"What I am doing may well be foolish but that doesn't make *me* a fool!"

"I am sorry that people think I am wrong for doing this thing, but that is only a disadvantage and is hardly the end of the world!"

"I know exactly why I am doing this act that I consider shameful, and therefore I can view it differently and see that it may be peculiar but that doesn't mean that I am a peculiar or *incompetent person*. I am just a *person who* is choosing to act strangely in this instance."

Do this shame-attacking exercise and preferably do it many times until you feel thoroughly unashamed of doing it and even feel comfortable with it. Observe how your feelings and attitudes about "shameful" acts distinctly change as you keep doing these exercises.

CHAPTER 14

Insight No. 9: Using Work and Practice

In my book, *Reason and Emotion in Psychotherapy,* I pointed out that RET includes three main insights, which are quite different from psychoanalytic insight.[1] The first two RET insights are:

1. You largely upset yourself at point C (Consequences), and do not really *get* upset by others or by events, at point A (Activating Events), and you do so by accepting or inventing irrational Beliefs (iBs).

2. No matter when, how, and why you originally made yourself anxious or depressed, you remain so today because you *still* consciously or unconsciously hold iBs.

We have been talking about and expanding these RET insights so far and have added the insight that although as a child you were limited in your ability to see and change your irrational Beliefs, you now have considerable ability to do so—if you *see* and *use* the eight expanded insights discussed in the previous pages.

We now proceed to RET's original Insight No. 3, which in our expanded version we shall call *Insight No. 9: No matter how clearly you see that you upset yourself and make yourself needlessly miserable, you rarely will improve except through work and practice—yes, considerable work and practice—to actively change your disturbance-creating Beliefs and to vigorously (and often uncomfortably) act against them.*

Insight No. 9 presents the Achilles heel (and the Catch-22) of all therapies, including RET. For it is easy for you to adopt and create self-defeating philosophies and to embed them into your actions and inactions. Damned easy! Because you tend to unconsciously and effortlessly make yourself miserable. In fact, in addition to your self-actualizing tendencies, you have a fine talent for self-defeat. Alas!

Insight No. 9 of RET tells you that, yes—definitely, yes—you *can* work to change your miserable thoughts, feelings and behaviors. But it doesn't necessarily make it *easy* to do so!

However, *Insight No. 9* at least gives you a good chance to change. For it clearly states that if you are willing to work and practice—and to *continue* to work and practice—to surrender your irrational Beliefs and actions, you will most likely (I would say you are about 98 percent likely) to make yourself much less miserable.

Insight No. 9 shows how RET differs from most other awareness-oriented psychotherapies. For several cognitive therapies were devised before RET—for example, those of Pierre Janet, Emile Coué, Paul Dubois, and Alfred Adler.[2]

But these intellectual therapies fail to stress behavioral methods of changing personality. They often forget that to change your ideas, you had better persistently work at doing so—since you are born and reared to think crookedly and to unconsciously slip into rigid *shoulds* and *musts*. Even when you clearly *see* your *must*urbation and therefore give it up, you easily fall back, again and again, to dogmatic thinking.

Moreover, unless you repeatedly *act* against a phobic belief, you rarely eliminate it. If you are anxious about making friendly overtures to someone and you avoid making them, every time you "escape" from this "fearful" situation, you unconsciously reinforce your phobia. By running away, you really tell yourself, whether or not you realize what you are thinking, "It *would* be awful if I were rejected! I must be *sure* I will be accepted before I try again." So you become more afraid.

On the other hand, if you keep making friendly overtures in spite of your horror of rejection, you usually see that nothing "horrible" happens, and you greatly help yourself overcome your phobia.

If we wish to put most neurotic problems under two main headings, we can call them (1) ego disturbance (self-damning) and (2) low frustration tolerance (LFT) or discomfort disturbance. Ego disturbance arises when you strongly believe, "*I* must do well and win others' approval, and *I* am an inadequate, undeserving person when I don't do as well as I *must*." This is really grandiosity—since you are demanding that you be *special, outstanding, perfect, superhuman*—which, of course, you will rarely be!

Discomfort disturbance is also godlike, because the main philosophy behind it is: "Since I am such a special person who *needs* to have my main wants and interests gratified, other people *must* give me exactly what I desire and conditions *must* be nicely arranged to cater to my wishes. If not, it's *awful,* I *can't stand it,* and life is hardly worth living!"[3]

So one major idea leading to discomfort disturbance is: "My life *must* be easy and people *have to* give me everything I truly crave." This can then lead to a related irrational Belief: "In order to make my life completely satisfying, I *must* always do well and *have to* win the love of all significant people all the time!" These ideas create low frustration tolerance (LFT). But they also involve ego because they insist that "*I* must have an easy life, *I* must be perfect, and people and conditions should always cater to *me, me, me, me!*"

Why is LFT so important in therapy? Because no matter how you originally disturb yourself, when you know you are upset, know your upsetting Beliefs, know what you can probably do about them, and still refuse to work at upsetting yourself, you almost always are a victim of your own LFT. If you know, for example, that you feel uncomfortable going for job interviews and, especially, being turned down for a job; and if you realize that you have irrational Beliefs that escalate your discomfort and pain into great anxiety, you can overcome your anxiety by using RET to strongly convince yourself that you *can* stand being rejected and that your discomfort is *inconvenient* but hardly *awful.* But you will have to *work* hard at convincing yourself of these sane ideas when you forcefully believe the crazy ones.

You had better, therefore, *use* your knowledge of how to change your ideas that create your anxiety; and you had better *keep working at using it* until you overcome your anxiety and rarely bring it back. You had also better force yourself, no matter how uncomfortable you are, to go on many job interviews, until you become less and less panicked about them.

When you indulge in your anxiety instead of making real efforts to overcome it, you are giving in to your LFT or discomfort disturbance. And when you temporarily make yourself unanxious but then refuse to keep doing so, you are also indulging in LFT.

Low frustration tolerance, then, often leads to anxiety and depression. But even more often it encourages you to maintain your disturbed feelings when you could let them go. To reduce LFT, you had better make yourself do many difficult tasks *now, pronto,* no matter how you *feel* about doing them.

Do, don't stew! And don't wait until you feel in the mood to do so. Strike while the spirit is cold!

Isn't this Catch-22: To try to overcome your LFT—which stems from the idea that working to overcome it *shouldn't* require real effort—by pushing your rump to do "overly" hard things? Yes, it is. But don't forget that Catch-22 stems from an idea in your head and doesn't really exist in itself. And if it is mainly a thought—RET clearly says—you can overcome it by debating and Disputing it!

The contradiction leading to Catch-22 about LFT is:

1. "I shouldn't have to work very hard to get what I want, even though I will benefit in the long run by doing so. It's *too* hard to really work for my own happiness. I need immediate gratification."

2. The only way to get over my LFT and become a long-range, sane hedonist is to work hard to overcome my prejudice against working hard!

The rational answer that you can use to overcome this paradox is: "Yes, it's quite hard to work to get what I want and to delay immediate gratification in order to derive future pleasure. But it's considerably hard*er* if I don't! Short-range gain will often bring me long-lived pain in the future! Too bad—but that's the way it often is. Sure I have to exert myself to overcome my LFT— but I'll require *more* effort, leading to *prolonged* pain, if I don't overcome it."

"Nobody promised me a rose garden. If I insist that they do, I'll only end up with extra thorns!"

Back to RET's *Insight No. 9*. Almost always there's no way but work and practice—w-o-r-k and p-r-a-c-t-i-c-e—to eradicate, and to keep away your emotional misery. Insight by itself is not enough. Nor will you get too far by merely acknowledging and expressing your feelings.

You had better *also* challenge and Dispute your irrational Beliefs a thousand times. Arrive at rational Beliefs and forcefully get them into your head a thousand times. Get in touch with, feel, and sometimes express your feelings a thousand times. Act against your disturbed thoughts and emotions a thousand times. And then, if necessary, a thousand more times! For many months, sometimes for years. Sometimes, off and on, for the rest of your life!

We can state *Insight No. 9* differently: There is no magical, easy way of changing yourself. Optimism and hope won't do it. Prayer and supplication won't do it. Getting support and love from others won't do it. Even reading this book won't do it! All these things may help you *feel* better. Some of them will show you what to do to *get* better. But in the final analysis, only *you* can make yourself change. You and the persistent *work* you do. Work? Yes, *work!*

You can stop feeling severely anxious, depressed, and otherwise miserable by employing RET principles of work and practice in two main ways:

1. Use *several* thinking, feeling, and action RET techniques— such as those explained in this book and other RET writings. Give each one a fair chance. If one doesn't work, use another, and another, and another! And if one does work, keep trying some of the other RET techniques, too.

2. Keep using each RET method many times. Even when one of them—such as singing rational human songs to yourself—works beautifully for a while, employ it again and again until you sink its message into your head and into your bones. Overlearn it. And from time to time, keep reviewing it—lest you forget, lest you forget!

Pablo, a forty-year-old travel agent, understood the principles and practice of RET very well, and frequently used them with his close friends and with the volunteers at my regular Friday night Workshop in Problems of Daily Living, to whom he often gave excellent rational suggestions after I interviewed them about their emotional problems. But whenever Pablo made himself very angry at others—which was several times a week—he let his rage boil for over an hour, sometimes for the entire day, before he used RET to overcome it and allow himself to go back to writing the great American play.

Because of his knowledge of RET, Pablo knew how he created his fury with irrational Beliefs: "People *shouldn't* act so damned stupidly! What hopeless idiots they are!" And: "My wife, who keeps saying that she loves me, *must not* be so selfish and uncaring! What a rotten hypocrite she is!"

Pablo also often recognized his secondary disturbance and the irrational Beliefs behind it. He knew that he hated *himself* whenever he had a furious outburst at *others*. And he tracked down his self-damning ideas: "I *should* know better than to bring on this childish rage! What a fool I am for not using RET to eliminate it! How disgusting!"

In spite of his insight into how he kept needlessly enraging and downing himself, Pablo frequently indulged in both these miserable feelings—and kept ruining his playwriting and his relationships. On several occasions, he got into fistfights with "horribly stupid" people. His wife kept leaving him because of his outbursts against her and others. And his plays never got finished. Still he refused to use RET to overcome his rage and self-hatred.

After many failures to do his RET homework, Pablo worked out the following plan with his therapy group:

For one month, he would devote at least two hours a day to using—not merely understanding but *using*—RET. He would especially work at fully accepting himself no matter how many times he foolishly enraged himself against others:

1. He would spend at least ten minutes every day actively Disputing his irrational Beliefs, "I *should* know better than to bring on this foolish rage! What a fool I am for not using RET to eliminate it! How disgusting!"

2. He would persist at this Disputing until he fully accepted himself *with* his foolish behavior.

3. He would very strongly repeat to himself, at least fifteen times each day, the rational Belief, "Because I am a fallible human, I will often act stupidly and at times *continue* to foolishly enrage myself. Too damned bad!"

4. He would make a list of the disadvantages of damning himself for *anything,* and read and think about this list at least five times each day.

5. He would do at least one RET shame-attacking exercise daily—force himself to do what he considered a "shameful" or "stupid" act in public (such as singing at the top of his lungs in the subway) and work at *not*—yes, *not*—feeling humiliated or downed when he did it.

6. He would sing to himself several times a day one of the rational humorous songs which rips up perfectionism and self-downing, such as these songs:[4]

PERFECT RATIONALITY
(Tune, Luigi Denza, *Funiculi, Funicula*)

Some think the world must have a right direction,
And so do I! And so do I!
Some think that, with the slightest imperfection

They can't get by—and so do I!
For I, I have to prove I'm superhuman,
And better far than people are!
To show I have miraculous acumen—
And always rate among the Great.
Perfect, perfect rationality
Is, of course, the only thing for me!
How can I ever think of being
If I must live fallibly?
Rationality must be a perfect thing for me!

BEAUTIFUL HANGUP
(Tune, Stephen Foster, *Beautiful Dreamer*)

Beautiful hangup, why should we part
When we have shared our whole lives from the start?
We are so used to taking one course
Oh, what a crime it would be to divorce!
Beautiful hangup, don't go away!
Who will befriend me if you do not stay?
Though you still make me look like a jerk,
Living without you would take so much work!
Living without you would take so much work!

I AM BAD, OH SO BAD!
(Tune, Anton Dvorak, *Going Home*,
from *The New World Symphony*)

I am bad, oh so bad, just a worthless cad!
Oh, my gad! Let me add: I'm so bad it's sad!
I'm so bad I deserve every ugly twist!
I'm so bad I've a nerve even to exist!
I'm so bad that I'm clad in pure villainy!
Oh, I'm so bad, you egad
Must take care of me!
Yes, take care of me!
Yes, take care of me!

(Lyrics by Albert Ellis, copyright © 1977 to 1980 by Institute for Rational-Emotive Therapy)

As he worked—and worked and worked!—on his secondary symptom of damning himself for his rage and for not trying hard enough to give up his fury, Pablo also worked on his primary symptom of rage. He took his irrational Beliefs that people *shouldn't* be so stupid and that his wife *must* be less selfish and more caring and (with the help of his therapy group) planned these RET homework assignments:

1. He spent at least ten minutes a day actively and vigorously Disputing his irrational Beliefs.

2. He forcefully told himself rational coping statements, at least fifteen times a day, such as: "People *should* often act stupidly—because that is their nature!" "My wife *will be* at times selfish and uncaring—and has a perfect right to be more interested in herself than in me!"

3. He penalized himself by burning a hundred dollar bill every time he got into a fistfight with someone and every time he screamed at his wife.

4. He practiced rational emotive imagery at least once a day by imagining that people were really acting stupidly, letting himself feel very angry about this, and then working on feeling *only* disappointed and frustrated, but *not* angry, about their stupid behavior.

5. He sang to himself every day—and really thought about—several rational humorous songs poking fun at feelings of anger, such as these two popular songs, to which I have put new rational lyrics:

LOVE ME, LOVE ME, ONLY ME!
(Tune, *Yankee Doodle*)

Love me, love me, only me or I'll die without you!
Make your love a guarantee, so I can never doubt you!
Love me, love me totally; really, really try, dear;
But if you demand love, too, I'll hate you till I die, dear!
Love me, love me all the time, thoroughly and wholly;
Life turns into slush and slime 'less you love me solely!
Love me with great tenderness, with no ifs or buts, dear.
If you love me somewhat less I'll hate your goddamned guts, dear!

GLORY, GLORY HALLELUJAH!
(Tune, *Battle Hymn of the Republic*)

Mine eyes have seen the glory of relationships that glow
And then falter by the wayside as love passions come—and go!
I've heard of great romances where there is no slightest lull—
But I am skeptical!

Glory, glory, hallelujah! People love ya till they screw ya!
If you'd cushion how they do ya, then don't expect they won't!

Glory, glory Hallelujah! People cheer ya—then pooh-pooh ya!
If you'd soften how they screw ya,
Then don't expect they won't!

(Lyrics by Albert Ellis, copyright © 1977 by Institute for Rational-Emotive Therapy)

Pablo did a good job of carrying out these thinking, feeling, and activity assignments. And when at times he failed to do his RET homework, he worked hard at refusing to blame himself for failing. He only criticized his *performance* but not his *self*, his *totality*.

As a result of this RET homework program, Pablo cut down his temper tantrums to a few times a month. Whenever he did have them, he quickly admitted that he had upset himself and indulged in his rage for only five or ten minutes. Then he found his irrational demands that made him angry and succeeded in actively Disputing and surrendering them in a few minutes. He occasionally slipped and let himself rage for an hour or more. But he usually continued his outbursts for no more than ten minutes—and often for only two or three.

Pablo was very happy about the time and energy he saved by his anti-anger program. He no longer wasted hours indulging in his rages and his sulking, and he was able to devote much more time every week to writing his play.

You will find no panacea when you work and practice at changing your self-sabotaging ideas and behaviors. Telling yourself that you *must* work hard at therapy and *have to* keep practicing RET can even be harmful. And *seeing* how you upset yourself and how you can stop doing so is not enough. *Using* RET and forcefully *striving* to minimize your misery is the key. Not a magical but a practical key to stubbornly refusing to make yourself miserable about anything. Yes, anything!

RET Exercise No. 14

For the exercise, you can write out an RET sheet for Disputing Irrational Beliefs (DIBS), the instructions for which are given in *A New Guide for Rational Living* and in a separate pamphlet on "Techniques for Disputing Irrational Beliefs," issued by the Institute for Rational-Emotive Therapy.[1] To do this, take one of your

irrational Beliefs (iBs) and ask yourself several important challenging questions about it, until you really give it up and strongly
believe—and *feel* that it is false.

The questions that you use in DIBS are these:

1. What irrational Belief (iB) do I want to Dispute and surrender?

2. Can I rationally prove this Belief?

3. What evidence can I find to disprove this Belief?

4. Does any evidence exist for the truth of this Belief?

5. What are the worst things that could *actually* happen to me if
I give up this Belief and act against it?

6. What good things could happen or could I make happen if I
give up this Belief?

If you have low frustration tolerance about doing RET and working hard and persistently at it until you begin to change your disturbed thoughts, feelings, and behaviors, you might use this DIBS
to change your LFT:

1. WHAT IRRATIONAL BELIEF (iB) DO I WANT TO
DISPUTE AND SURRENDER?

Illustrative Answer: "I must not have to work hard at changing
myself with RET. It should come easy! It's much *too* hard to go to
all that trouble. How *awful* that someone won't do it for me!"

2. CAN I RATIONALLY PROVE OR SUPPORT THIS BE-
LIEF?

Illustrative Answer: No.

3. WHAT EVIDENCE CAN I FIND TO DISPROVE THIS
BELIEF?

Illustrative Answer: Considerable evidence, such as:

(a) There is no reason why I *must* not have to work hard at
changing myself with RET. If hard work were not required,
changing myself would be very easy. But, obviously, it's not
easy! So it looks like I'd better acknowledge that *if* I want to
change, I'd damn well better work persistently and hard to do
so!

(b) Where is it written that changing myself by using RET
should or ought to come easy? Only in my grandiose wishes and
in my silly head! No matter how desirable it is for me to change
easily, my desire for ease does not automatically bring it on.

(c) How is it *too* hard for me to go to the trouble of changing myself with RET? It surely is not *impossibly* hard, though it may be *very* hard. To call it "too hard" is for me to resort to magical thinking, for I really mean that it is harder than I want it to be and therefore it is "too" hard. But this means that I say that whatever I want to be easy must really be easy—that I run the blasted universe! Well, *do* I? Hardly!

(d) Yes, it is really hard for me to change by using RET, but right now it *should be* that hard—for that's the way it really is: truly difficult. So it is! Tough! But no matter how tough I find it to be, it *still* is that hard.

(e) Yes, it's hard for me to change but I'd better face the fact that it's much hard*er* if I don't. For then I keep my usual anxiety and depression, and probably keep it forever. Look how hard *that* is!

(f) Where is the evidence that it is *awful* if someone doesn't make me easily change or do my RET for me and thus make me change! It's not *awful*, because *awful*, in the sense I'm using it, means *more than* bad; and it may be bad, or inconvenient, that I have to work at the RET to change myself, but that inconvenience is hardly 101 percent or 120 percent bad. Not even 99 percent. And the badder I see it, the more exaggerated badness that I give to it, the *more* frustrated I'll feel and the more I'll interfere with my using RET to change myself. So I'd better see it as *just* bad or inconvenient.

4. DOES ANY EVIDENCE EXIST FOR THE TRUTH OF MY IRRATIONAL BELIEF, "I MUST NOT HAVE TO WORK HARD AT CHANGING MYSELF WITH RET"?

Illustrative Answer: "None that I can see. There is a good deal of evidence that it *is* hard to work at changing myself with RET and that it right now *should* be hard (because it realistically is!). But although it would be very fortunate if I could easily and quickly change, just by knowing RET and thinking about how good it is, that kind of good fortune just doesn't exist in the world. If I *presently* work hard at using RET, I may *later* find it easy and automatic to do so. But at the present time it's hard because it's hard! So, having no better resource, I'd better do the work it entails gracefully, without creating for myself an even *bigger* hassle about it!

5. WHAT ARE THE WORST THINGS THAT COULD AC-
TUALLY HAPPEN TO ME IF I GIVE UP THE BELIEF THAT
IT'S TOO HARD TO WORK AT CHANGING MYSELF WITH
RET?

Illustrative Answer:

(a) I would keep working at RET and that would be a real pain
in the neck. So it would be a pain in the neck! But if I don't work
at it, I would continue to have all the hassles and troubles I do
have—and I would presumably have them forever!

(b) IF I don't use RET and don't work at it to get over my
problems, they will not only remain, but they will most probably
increase. That will be even worse. But even if I do nothing and
my problems increase, it will *only* be uncomfortable and inconvenient. It still will not be *awful*—that is, badder than it *should*
be, and *more than* bad. It will only be bad!

(c) If I work at RET, the worst that could really happen would
be that I still won't improve at all, so all my work would therefore be wasted. But at least I would then know that I had *tried* to
do my best to get better. This way, without working and without
trying, I will never even know how much better I could get—or
could not get. So I had better make the effort and see how well I
can do.

(d) Even if I work hard at RET and never get better at all, I
could then still live with my frustration and my pain. This is
unlikely—for if I work I most likely will improve to some degree.
But if I never improve one bit, I don't. Whatever happens—or
does not happen—to me in life is *still* only a bother, still only an
inconvenience. And if I stop whining and screaming *about* that
inconvenience, that in itself will save me gratuitous, *extra* bothering of myself. So I'd still better do the work.

6. WHAT GOOD THINGS MIGHT HAPPEN OR MIGHT I
MAKE HAPPEN IF I WORK AT USING RET IN REGARD TO
MY PROBLEMS?

Illustrative Answer:

(a) I might really get over my problem by using RET. I'm now
anxious and depressed and by using RET I could well become
considerably less anxious and depressed. Or even *un*anxious and
*un*depressed!

(b) If I overcome my low frustration tolerance in this area I will tend to become more generally disciplined and may well overcome my LFT in various other areas of my life, such as overeating and procrastination.

(c) It is a great challenge for me to enjoy life while working hard to use RET and while giving up present pleasures for future gains. The challenge of not upsetting myself while I am going through some amount of deprivation is one of the best challenges that I can take in life.

(d) By working against my low frustration tolerance, even if it takes me a while to succeed, I will get better and better at it, can at times *enjoy* my activity, and can see that I am increasingly promoting my *own* independence and emotional mastery. What could be more rewarding than running my *own* life?

CHAPTER 15

Insight No. 10: Forcefully Changing Your Beliefs and Behaviors

You can express thoughts, feelings, and behaviors lightly or strongly, mildly or forcefully—as you can easily observe. You can feel mildly or intensely sad about a loss. You can exercise vigorously or gently. You can be greatly or moderately addicted to smoking or overeating.

Can thoughts, too, be weak or strong?

Robert Abelson, Robert Zajonc, and other psychologists say yes. As Abelson pointed out a number of years ago, you can have "cool" and "hot" cognitions.[1] According to RET, your "hot" thoughts influence you more and create more intense feelings than do your "cool" thoughts.

Thus, if you have to pass an exam to get a job, you may have a cool thought: "Jobs like this frequently require a test." Your cool, descriptive thought will lead to your having little or no feeling.

You may also have a warm or preferential thought—which in RET we call a rational Belief—about the test and the job: "I definitely want to pass this test and get this job and since the test doesn't seem too hard, I like taking it." This warm thought will probably lead you to feel optimistic and help you do well on the test.

You may finally have a hot or highly evaluative thought: "I *have* to pass this test and get this job in order to enjoy life at all and to accept myself as a good person! If the test is harder than it seems and I fail it, that would be *awful* and would prove that I'm a schnook who will never get a decent job!" This is a hot thought—an irrational Belief in RET—that will very likely make you feel intense anxiety and interfere with your doing well on the test.

131

RET also states that you hold some hot thoughts very strongly, rigidly, and forcefully, while you hold some lightly and less vividly.[2] You may believe that you must pass a test and are a real clod if you don't and may believe this (1) occasionally or always; (2) loosely or devoutly; (3) mildly or intensely; (4) blandly or vividly; (5) softly or loudly; (5) in a limited way (about one situation) or generally (about many situations).

As you can see, your hot thoughts include many kinds of heat! RET also holds that you create more intense feelings—and particularly disturbed feelings—with your hot than with your warm thoughts. Hot thinking often encourages you to have self-defeating emotions and behaviors that persist longer and are harder for you to change.

If you fanatically believe that you must *always* pass important tests and get *every single* job for which you apply, and you also believe that you are a *hopeless nincompoop* when you *in any way* fail, you will tend to make yourself extremely anxious when you go for a test or a job interview. This anxiety may disrupt your whole life, and you will have one heck of a time relieving it. Moreover, you will often feel such intense panic and discomfort that you may well make yourself terrified about it. You then bring on strong secondary symptoms of anxiety about your anxiety.

Because your hot thoughts create intense and lasting anxiety and depression, you had better acquire *Insight No. 10: If you mildly Dispute your irrational Beliefs (iBs) you may not change them and keep them changed. Therefore, you had better powerfully and persistently argue against them and persuade yourself that they are false.*

When, for example, you ask yourself—at point D, Disputing of your iBs—"Why *must* I always pass important tests?" you had better very vigorously (and *often*) reply: "I *don't* have to do so! I'd love to pass and will work hard to do so. But if I don't, I don't! I definitely *want* this job, but I never, never *need* it. I *can* be happy if I don't get it, though not *as* happy as if I do. I *can* pass other tests and other jobs even if I fail at getting this one. I will only be a *person who* failed this time, and clearly not a *hopeless failure!*"

RET says that the more emphatically and the more frequently you challenge and debate your red-hot negative thoughts, the quicker and more completely you will kill them—and the more you will reduce (and *keep* away) the disturbed feelings which they create.

So back to *Insight No. 10*: When you track down your iBs that make you anxious (and that panic you *about* your anxiety), you can become a *passionate* scientist who strongly comes up with rational answers to your irrational Beliefs.

Take Tom, for example. Although tall and handsome, aged thirty-five, and a successful physician, he kept falling madly in love with fine women—and quickly turned them all off. They found him too insecure, too needy. As I often ask my clients, who *needs* a needy person? Not Tom's women friends!

Tom understood RET and knew exactly what he was telling himself to make himself shaky when he met a charming woman: "I love her so strongly and would feel so deprived if she did not return my feelings that I *absolutely must* win her. I *have to*! I've *got to*! I *must*!"

Noting this kind of *must*urbation and seeing that it didn't work, Tom used RET to try to give it up, and kept asking himself, "Why *must* I win this woman I care for? Do I really *have to* please her? Would I *die* without her love?"

He gave the correct, rational answers to these Disputations and helped himself somewhat. For a while. But then he fell right back to his great need. And to his insecurity.

I gave Tom the RET homework assignment of having a *forceful* rational dialogue with himself and recording the dialogue. He tried to do so and brought me in a cassette tape in which he nicely Disputed his iBs about winning the love of a special woman, but when I and members of his therapy group listened to it, we found his arguments good—but his tone wishy-washy. He *knew* the rational words to combat his neediness; but he obviously didn't *believe* them.

So I had Tom do the tape over, asking him to be much *harder* on his irrational Beliefs.

No dice. His second tape dialogue was only a bit stronger in tone than his first one. And he still remained a love slob.

His third tape was much better. Part of it went as follows:

Tom's Irrational Voice: If Cora, who's just about the best woman I have met in years, doesn't really love me, what decent woman will? None!

Tom's Rational Voice: None? What crap! With so many fine women I could meet? Obviously, *some* would care for me. Even if they were stupid for doing so!

Tom's Irrational Voice: But suppose they only cared because they were stupid. That would show what an unlovable jerk I am!

Tom's Rational Voice: To hell it would! At worst, it would show that I am sadly lacking some good traits. But never that I am totally unlovable. Nor would it show, if no woman found me desirable, that I would be a *complete jerk*. I would just be a loser in *that* area.

Tom's Irrational Voice: Yes, the most important of *all* areas. That would really make you one damned loser!

Tom's Rational Voice: No—a loser in *love*. But not in *every* area. Not in *life*! A loser to fine women. But not, dammit, to me!

Tom's Irrational Voice: There you go—rationalizing again! What good is your life if you can't have real love? So you'll be a great physician. Hah!

Tom's Rational Voice: Yes—I hope—a great physician. And great at sports! And a fine reader! I have lots of things I can really enjoy—even if I never find a good partner.

Tom's Irrational Voice: Never? Never?

Tom's Rational Voice: Yes, never! Immanuel Kant never mated—or probably ever even dated. And he had a good life! Many other outstanding people, too, were happy without love. But whether they were or not, *I'm* going to be! Just as soon as I stop whining about my being "unlovable"!

As soon as Tom learned the knack of *vigorously, powerfully* Disputing his own irrational Beliefs—which he now referred to as his Bullshit—he began to do so many times. I and the members of his therapy group didn't have to tell him, after he recorded a dialogue like the one above, that it was strong enough. His *feeling* of immense relief from anxiety and depression showed him that it was. He *immediately* felt he didn't *need* (though he still keenly *desired*) love. And he felt that way for the next few weeks.

As Tom kept fiercely arguing himself out of being a love slob, he felt much less needy. Four months later, he was almost totally cured—and consequently the women he dated often wanted to continue seeing him—and some highly desirable ones tried to cart him off to the altar! A year later, he started to live with the one he liked best and three years later he married her. He is now teaching her how to actively—and quite vigorously—talk herself out of some of her own emotional Bullshit.

RET Exercise No. 15

Take one of your irrational Beliefs that you really want to give up, because you know that you are seriously defeating yourself by holding it, and dispute it both mildly or moderately, on the one hand, and vigorously or powerfully on the other hand. You may do this by writing out the irrational Belief and then making one column of mild disputings and changing of it, and one column of vigorous disputings and changing. Or, better yet, you can take a tape recorder, record your irrational Belief on it, and then have a dialogue with yourself on the recorder, in the course of which you moderately *and* powerfully dispute this Belief until you really feel that you have made some real progress in giving up and changing it to a set of strong rational philosophies.

A sample of your written out Disputing might go as follows:

IRRATIONAL BELIEF: I really have to pass this test that I am about to take because if I don't, my whole career will go down the drain and I'll surely end up working all my life in some menial capacity and making very little money and that would be absolutely horrible! What a worm I would then be!

Instead of, or in addition to, disputing your irrational Belief powerfully and vigorously on paper (as in the above illustration), you can have both a mild and a forceful dialogue with yourself on a tape recorder, and make sure that you end up by believing and feeling the forceful arguments that you present on the tape. Take this self-dialogue, for example:

Mild Disputing and Rational Answer	*Powerful Disputing and Rational Answer*
If I fail this test I can take other tests and pass them later. So why worry?	Even if I fail the test and every other test I still can get a good job doing something. And if I don't, I don't! I can still be happy.

Mild Disputing and Rational Answer	*Powerful Disputing and Rational Answer*
My whole career won't go down the drain. I'll just be slower at getting what I want in the course of it.	If my whole damned career went down the drain, I could still get another enjoyable and well-paying career!
I'll sooner or later probably pass this test and get some kind of a decent career.	I'll darned well pass this test one of these days, probably this time! And whether or not I do, I'm absolutely determined to get a good career!
If I keep working in a menial capacity it won't kill me.	Whatever capacity I keep working in, I am determined to get some very good things out of the work. And even if I never do enjoy it, I can always find other aspects of my life that will be exceptionally enjoyable!
If I make very little money all my life, I can still get by.	If I make very little money all my life, I cannot only get by but somehow manage to have a damned good time. Money is important but it clearly isn't everything!
It would be pretty inconvenient to make little money all my life, but it wouldn't be the end of the world.	It would be damned inconvenient to make little money all my life, but in one way or another I will work my butt off to make more. If somehow I don't succeed, I will merely reduce my expenses and be one of the happiest people alive who lives on very little!
If I fail this test and make less money for the rest of my life, I'll only be a person who failed but not a rotten worm.	No matter how many tests I fail or how little money I make in life, I am never a worm or a totally incompetent person. I am and will always be a fallible human; but I can always fully accept myself and look for every possible pleasure in life no

Mild Disputing and *Rational Answer*	*Powerful Disputing and* *Rational Answer*
	matter how badly I act in certain respects. I am I; and just because I am alive and am myself I ALWAYS deserve to have the best time I can have during my lifetime. Now how the hell do I manage to have that good time? By striving for it!

IRRATIONAL BELIEF: My friend, Norbert, borrowed money from me and said that he'd pay it back quickly. Now several months have gone by and he still hasn't paid it. What is more, he's acting as if I just gave him the money as a gift and that he's not supposed to pay it back. If he gets a lot of money, he says, he will give me back what I lent him, but just out of the goodness of his heart and not because he really owes it to me. How could he do a thing like that to me?! What a thorough bastard he is! This means that he has no real good qualities. He deserves to be severely damned and punished, and I think I'll really get back at him. I'll show him that he can't act that way to me!"

ILLUSTRATIVE DIALOGUE:

Irrational You: How could he do a thing like that?

Mild Answer: He just could. That's the way he often behaves just like that. Well, that's his problem.

Strong Answer: He damned well easily could do a thing like that! It's not the first time he's acted that way and I'll bet it won't be the last! I wish to hell that he wouldn't be like that, but he often is. Tough! But I can expect it—and take it!

Irrational You: But after all I did for him! I went out of my way to lend him the money and he *still* insists that I gave it to him! What a thorough bastard he is!

Mild Answer: Yes, I really went out of my way to lend him the money, but that doesn't mean that he has to go out of his way to pay me back. He's not a thorough bastard—though he sometimes acts in a bastardly manner.

Strong Answer: Yes, I went out of my way to lend him the money, but that never in the least means that he has to go out of his way, or to be very honest, and to pay it back. Whatever I decide to do is *me*; and what he decides to do is *Norbert*. Well, that certainly is a rotten thing for him to do, and I definitely won't trust him in the future—or lend him any *more* money! But he's not a thorough bastard—not even an *un*thorough bastard. He's just a fallible human, like all of us are; and this is one of his great fallibilities. Well, I'll never like his having this kind of failing, but I can clearly live with it, still try to get my money back, and be a happy human—though not *as* happy—if I never get it. Isn't it too darned bad that some of my best "friends" turn out to be unfriendly?

Irrational You: I still think he's a thorough bastard! If he can do a thing like this, he has no real good qualities.

Mild Answer: Isn't that an exaggeration on my part? Of course, he, like all humans, has *some* good qualities. It's just this aspect of him that is bad.

Strong Answer: What nonsense! Of course he has good qualities, too. Everyone does. Even Hitler doubtless had a few. But for all his good qualities—and I'd better admit that at other times he has been quite good to me—his not accepting that he borrowed the money and falsely claiming that I gave it to him is really a bad *act*. And that's just what I'm going to try to show him—not that *he* is bad but that his dishonest *act* is. I'm really going to persist at trying to show him that. But if I can't, I can't. At worst, I'll just lose the money and cut him off as a friend.

Irrational You: Damned well I'll cut him off as a friend! Me, friendly with a person like that? Never! He deserves to be severely damned and punished, and I think I'll really get back at him.

Mild Answer: What's the use of getting back at him? I'll only waste more time doing that. I might as well drop it. But he really is a pretty crummy person.

Strong Answer: How silly of me to try to get back at him! I wasted enough time and money already in dealing with him and now I'm just going to continue this nonsense by thinking about him and wasting time and energy trying to get back at him. He may theoretically deserve, in a thoroughly just world, to be penalized for his bad behavior to me; but he hardly deserves to be severely damned and punished. No human is subhuman; no human is damnable. If I foolishly stole from him, the universe wouldn't spy on me and command that I must be damned and punished. Why, then, should he be? I'll still try to put pressure on him, but not angry pressure, to get my money back. But no waste of time damning him!

Irrational You: No matter how much time and energy it takes, I'll show him that he can't act that way to me. I'll fix his wagon! And, while I'm at it, maybe there's something I can do to get back at his wife and family, too!

Mild Answer: There's no way that I can certainly show him that he *can't* act that way to me. He has a right, as a human, to do whatever he wishes, even when he's clearly wrong. I'd better drop the whole thing and forget it.

Strong Answer: Of course, he *can* act that way to me. Damned well he can! In fact, he has a great talent for acting in that unfriendly way, and now that I've discovered this I'd better accept that grim reality. And I have no way, probably, of showing him that he can't act that way to me. No matter how vindictive I become, and even hurt his wife and family, that won't show him. In fact, it will probably show him, in his eyes, what a "louse" I am; and then he'll deliberately not pay the money back to me—and perhaps vindictively try to hurt me and my family. If I foolishly try to fix his wagon, I'll very likely fix my own wagon in the process. Then I'll suffer even *more* than I'm now suffering. What crap on my part! Just because he's wrong doesn't mean that I have to spend the rest of my life vindictively being wrong, too. Let me just try to talk to him, without anger and vindictiveness again, and see what I can do. And if I can't do anything, well, I just can't! I'd better still drop it. Yes, drop it and go about my own business!

When you have written out or done a tape recording on forcefully debating and disputing your irrational Belief about something, go over it to make it even stronger. Let some of your friends or associates go over it with you. Work on being strong but not violent. Try not to perpetuate the craziness in which you are engaging or that is being destructively used against you. Practice strongly, yes, s-t-r-o-n-g-l-y—disputing your own nutty ideas!

CHAPTER 16

Insight No. 11: Achieving Emotional Change Is Not Enough. Maintaining It Is Harder!

As Mark Twain said: "It's easy to quit smoking. I've done it a thousand times."

This sums up the history of dieting, too. For every hundred people who lose thirty pounds or more by various diets, well over ninety percent gain all or most of it back.

Similarly with psychotherapy. Millions of people change by going for therapy. But almost all of them at times fall back. For a while, their feelings of anxiety, depression, and rage disappear.

And then return!

Sometimes, if you work at erasing your emotional misery, you take two steps forward—and only one backwards. Sometimes the reverse. Sometimes you completely free yourself of depression. Then you fall right back in the thick black soup again. At times, you never experience an old problem—such as a fear of public speaking. But then you bring on an entirely new one—such as fear of job hunting.

This brings us to *Insight No. 11: You may for a while find it easy to change your feelings. But you'd better keep working, working, working to maintain your gains.*

Almost no person gets completely or forever cured of misery. Including you!

What can you do, then, to maintain your improvement and to deal with backsliding?

A great deal.

At the Institute for Rational-Emotive Therapy in New York City, we have given much thought to this question and have come up with a pamphlet that we give to all our clients.[1] Let me demonstrate *Insight No. 11* of RET by showing you some of the main points in this pamphlet, *How to Maintain and Enhance Your Rational-Emotive Therapy Gains.*

What are important things you can remember to maintain your improvement?

Try these:

1. When you fall back to old feelings of anxiety, depression, or self-downing, zero in on the exact thoughts, feelings, and behaviors you once changed to make yourself improve. If you again feel depressed, think back to how you previously used RET to make yourself undepressed. For example, you may remember that:

(a) You stopped telling yourself that you were worthless and that you couldn't ever succeed in getting what you wanted.

(b) You did well in a job and proved to yourself that you did have some ability to succeed.

(c) You forced yourself to go on interviews instead of avoiding them and thereby overcame your anxiety about them.

Remind yourself of thoughts, feelings, and behaviors that you have changed and that you have helped yourself by changing.

2. Keep thinking, thinking, and thinking rational Beliefs (rBs) or coping statements, such as: "It's great to succeed but I can fully accept myself as a person and enjoy life considerably even when I fail!" Don't merely parrot these statements but carefully *think* them many times. Yes, *strongly* think them through until you really begin to believe and feel that they are true.

3. Keep looking for, discovering, and disputing your irrational Beliefs (iBs) with which you are once again upsetting yourself. Take each important irrational Belief—such as, "I *have to* succeed in order to be a worthwhile person!"—and keep asking yourself: "Why is this belief true?" "Where is the evidence that my worth as a person depends on my succeeding?" "In what way would I be a rotten human if I failed at an important task?"

Keep forcefully disputing your irrational Beliefs whenever you see that you are letting them creep back again. And even when you are not bothering yourself, realize that you may bring them back. So ask yourself what you think they are, make yourself fully conscious of them—and vigorously dispute them.

4. Keep taking risks and doing things that you irrationally fear—

such as riding in elevators, socializing, job hunting, or creative writing. As you are overcoming one of your irrational fears, keep thinking *and* acting against it on a regular basis. *Do* what you are afraid to do—and very often!

If you feel uncomfortable when you force yourself to do things you irrationally fear, to hell with the discomfort! Don't allow yourself to cop out—and thereby to preserve your fears forever! Often, make yourself as uncomfortable as you can be, in order to erase your fears and to become unanxious and comfortable later.

5. Learn to clearly see the difference between appropriate bad feelings—such as those of sorrow, regret, and frustration, when you do not get some of the important things you want—and inappropriate bad feelings—such as those of depression, anxiety, self-hatred, and self-pity—when you are deprived. Whenever you feel *over*concerned (panicked) or *needlessly* miserable (depressed), admit that you are having a very common but an unhealthy feeling and that you are bringing it on yourself with some dogmatic *shoulds, oughts,* or *musts.*

Realize that you are quite capable of changing your inappropriate (or *must*urbatory) feelings back into appropriate (or preferential) ones. Get in touch with your depressed feelings and work on them until you *only* feel sorry and regretful. Get in touch with your anxious feelings and work on them until you *only* feel concerned and vigilant.

Use rational emotive imagery to vividly imagine unpleasant Activating Events even before they happen. Let yourself feel inappropriately upset (anxious, depressed, enraged, or self-downing) as you imagine them. Then work on your feelings to change them to appropriate emotions (concern, sorrow, annoyance, or regret) as you keep imagining some of the worst things happening. Don't give up until you actually do change your feelings.

6. Avoid procrastination. Do unpleasant tasks fast—today! If you still procrastinate, reward yourself with certain things that you enjoy—for example, eating, vacationing, reading, and socializing—only *after* you have performed the tasks that you easily avoid. If this won't work, give yourself a severe penalty—such as talking to a boring person for two hours or burning a hundred dollar bill—every time that you procrastinate.

7. Make an absorbing *challenge* and an *adventure* out of main-

taining your emotional health and keeping yourself reasonably happy no matter what kind of misfortunes assail you. Make the removal of your misery one of the most important things in your life—something you are utterly determined to achieve.

Fully acknowledge that you always have some *choice* about how to think, feel, and behave; and throw yourself actively into making that choice for yourself.

8. Remember—and use—the three main insights of RET that were first outlined in *Reason and Emotion in Psychotherapy* in 1962:

Insight No. 1: You largely *choose* to disturb yourself about the "upsetting" events of your life. You mainly *feel* the way you *think*. When obnoxious and frustrating things happen to you at point A (Activating Events), you consciously or unconsciously *select* rational Beliefs (rBs) that lead you to feel sad and regretful and you also *select* irrational Beliefs (iBs) that lead you to feel anxious, depressed, and self-hating.

Insight No. 2: No matter how or when you acquired your irrational Beliefs and habits, you now, in the present, *choose* to maintain them—and that is why you are *now* disturbed. Poor conditions (in the past and present) *affect* you; but they don't *disturb* you. Your present *philosophy* creates your *current* disturbance.

Insight No. 3: There is no magical way for you to change your personality and your strong tendencies to upset yourself. You really change with *work and practice*. *Your* work and *your* practice.

9. Keep looking—steadily but unfrantically—for personal pleasures and enjoyments—such as reading, entertainment, sports, hobbies, art, science, and other vital absorbing interests. Make your major life goal the achievement of emotional health—and also that of real enjoyment.

Try to become involved in a long-term purpose, goal, or interest in which you can remain truly absorbed. *Make* yourself a good, happy life by giving yourself something to live *for*. In that way you will distract yourself from serious woes and will help preserve your mental health.

10. Keep in touch with several other people who know something about RET and who can help review it with you. Tell them about your problems and let them know how you are using RET to overcome them. See if they agree with your solutions and can sug-

gest additional RET methods to work against your irrational Beliefs.

11. Practice using RET with some of your friends and associates who will let you try to help them with it. The more often you use it with others, and try to talk them out of their self-defeating ideas, the more you will understand the main principles of RET and be able to use them with yourself.

When you see other people irrational and upset, try to figure out—with or without talking to them about it—their main irrational Beliefs and how these can be actively and vigorously disputed. This, again, gives you practice in working on your own iBs.

12. Keep reading RET writings and listening to RET audio and audio-visual cassettes. Read and listen to several of these—particularly my books, *Humanistic Psychotherapy, A Guide to Personal Happiness, A New Guide to Rational Living,* and *Overcoming Procrastination,* as well as Paul Hauck's *Overcoming Depression* and Howard Young's *A Rational Counseling Primer.*[1]

Keep going back to this RET material, to remind yourself of some of the main rational-emotive ideas.

Georgiana, a thirty-four-year-old bookkeeper, came to RET because she was intensely jealous and angry when her husband David kept staring at attractive young women whenever they went out together. He denied doing this, but she insisted that he did and was convinced (to her horror) that every time he had sex with her he was really imagining some woman with enormous breasts (Georgiana had neat, small ones) that he had been staring at that day.

She became so upset about this that she often stopped having intercourse with him, just before the two of them were about to come to orgasm. This "drives me up the wall," he said. And although he loved and liked her, he was just about ready to leave.

Georgiana saw me for several sessions of individual RET and then joined one of my regular therapy groups for eight months. She realized that she was demanding that David only lust after her and never even think of another woman. She also saw that, even if he did at times stare at other women and think of them while having sex with her, that meant nothing about her own looks or sexiness. So she became only moderately jealous of David's interest in other women.

A few months later, however, Georgiana again became very jealous and insecure. So, as a homework assignment which she worked out with her therapy group, she spent several weeks reviewing and working on some of the points listed in the previous chapter of this book:

1. She reminded herself that one of the best means of overcoming her jealousy was refusing to connect her worth as a person with her *ability* to satisfy David sexually. She showed herself many times that she could accept herself fully even if she no longer greatly aroused him.

2. She forcefully kept telling herself the rational Belief (rB): "I *can* be loved by David and have a good marriage even if he *does* lust after women with big busts!"

3. She kept challenging and Disputing her irrational Belief (iB): "I *must* be the only truly exciting woman to David!"

4. She deliberately kept going with David to restaurants and other places where he was likely to see attractive women. She *assumed* he was staring at them and kept telling herself, "Tough!—that's the way he is: desiring other women. I can live with it!"

5. She saw the difference between her feeling *appropriately* sorry and *in*appropriately panicked and depressed when David stared at other women. She used rational-emotive imagery, imagined him eagerly staring, and made herself feel *only* sorry and disappointed, but *not* anxious and self-downing.

6. She noticed that she was making excuses for not viewing the Miss America beauty contest on TV. So she set herself a penalty of burning a ten dollar bill for every minute she avoided viewing it with David. She saw the entire contest and burned no money.

7. She gave herself the challenge of not only refusing to be miserable but actually enjoying her outings with David, even when she was sure he was staring at women with big breasts.

8. She repeated RET's original Insights No. 1, 2, and 3 to herself, especially No. 3: "Becoming less jealous requires *work and practice*. So I damned well had better keep working and working against my silly jealousy!"

9. She absorbed herself in the vital interest of designing and making her own clothes. She kept focusing on how well *they* looked rather than on how puny and "ugly" were her breasts.

10. She talked to a few of the group members and to her women friends who also knew RET and who kept helping her go back to using it when she slipped into jealous rages.

11. She used RET to help her friends and business associates (including her supervisor), and thus taught it better to herself.

12. She recorded her part of her group sessions and listened several times a week to the Disputing and advice that I and the other members used with her. She kept reading RET books and pamphlets, even though she had previously read them several times. She thereby kept reminding herself on points that she had half forgotten.

As a result of applying herself so strongly to RET maintenance practices, Georgiana got to the point where she rarely felt intense jealousy and rage. She was able, with the group's full consent, to quit therapy and keep working on her problem successfully to herself. She and her husband still come from time to time to my regular Friday night live demonstrations of RET. Her husband is most enthusiastic about her progress and has come to see one of our other therapists at the Institute for Rational-Emotive Therapy in New York to work on his anxiety about his job.

RET Exercise No. 16

Select some task that you would like to do and know that you preferably should do but you are avoiding or—at very best—are procrastinating on and therefore doing very slowly. For example:

Finishing a paper or a report.
Checking your monthly bank statement.
Doing your RET homework.
Making business calls, on the phone or in person.
Coming to work regularly on time.
Writing a new job resume.
Answering a long overdue letter to a friend.
Outlining a book you want to write.
Preparing to give a talk or a workshop.

Look for the things you are telling yourself to make yourself avoid or procrastinate. Especially:

Shoulds and musts: "I *shouldn't* have to do this difficult paper." "My RET homework *must* be easy to do."

Awfulizings: "It's *awful* to check this damned bank statement!" "It's *terrible* to make these blasted telephone calls!"

I-can't-stand-its: "I *can't stand* dressing to go to this party! I *can't bear* stupid parties like this one is sure to be!"

Too-hards: "It's not only hard to write this outline for a book. It's *too* hard! It's harder than it *should be!*"

Self-damning: "Because I'm not preparing this speech, as I *should* be, and because others prepare their speeches with no delays, there's something basically wrong with me, and that makes me an *incompetent person*. What a total idiot I am!"

Always and neverness: "Since I fell back at doing my RET, as I *must* not do, I'll *always* be no good at doing it and will *never* do it well."

Hopelessness: "Because I've been late to work a hundred times, as I *must* not be, it's *hopeless*, and I simply *can't* make myself be on time!"

Select some behavior or habit in which you are foolishly indulging even though you are harming yourself considerably by continuing to indulge in it. For example:

smoking cigarettes
overeating
telling yourself what a rotten person you are
drinking too much
overspending
doing pleasant tasks, like television viewing, instead of working on your RET homework
continuing to make yourself enraged at people's stupidities and inefficiencies
indulging in foolish phobias (such as avoiding using escalators or elevators)

Look for the things you are telling yourself to pander to immediate gratification and to make yourself addicted to harmful habits. Especially:

Shoulds and musts: Even though it's doing me great harm, I *must* have the relief of smoking this cigarette right now. I *absolutely need it* to relieve my tension.

Awfulizings: "It's *awful* that I just can't enjoy myself instead of working steadily at changing myself with RET! It's *terrible* that I must go through present pain to get later gain!"

I-can't-stand-its: "I *can't stand* pushing away this delicious food when it tastes so good! I need this extra food right now!"

Too-hards: "It's not merely hard for me to give up the pleasure and relaxation of booze and marijuana, it's much *too* hard! It *must* not be that hard!"

Self-damnings: "Because I'm not working my butt off at doing RET as I *ought* to be doing, and because I'm indulging instead in immediately enjoyable activities, as I *ought not* be doing, I'm a *pretty rotten* person who *deserves* to keep suffering."

Always and neverness: "Because I keep spending money on things I really do not need to get short-term pleasures that I foolishly think that I do need, I'll *never* change and will *always* be a stupid spendthrift!"

Hopelessness: "Because I have fallen back several times from doing my RET homework, and instead have taken the easier and instantly more gratifying path of not working at changing myself, it's *hopeless*. I *can't* stop indulging in easy things, so I might as well give in to my natural tendencies and forget about changing myself."

Once you look for and discover your irrational Beliefs (iBs) with which you are creating your low frustration tolerance and your indulgences, actively and vigorously dispute all your shoulds, oughts, musts, your awfulizings, your I-can't-stand-its, your too-hards, your self-damnings, your always and neverances, and your conclusions of hopelessness. For example:

Disputing: "Why *must* my RET homework be easy to do? Why *shouldn't* I have a hard time doing it and continuing to do it?"

Answer: "There's no reason why it should be easy, and several reasons why it should be hard: (1) Because it *is* hard. (2) Because I'm not yet used to doing it, and it may well become easier as I *continue* to do it. (3) Because it's natural for me to act foolishly, and at times highly *un*natural for me to act sensibly. So I'd better keep acting well, until I make it more 'natural.' "

Disputing: "What makes it *awful* to keep checking my damned bank account?"

Answer: "Nothing makes it *awful*, since it's only, in itself, a real nuisance. Only *I* make it *awful*—by foolishly *defining* it in this way. So I'd better stop that nonsense and *only* see it as it actually is—a required pain in the neck!"

Disputing: Where is the evidence that it's *too* hard for me to give up the pleasure and relaxation of booze and marijuana? Prove that it *must* not be that hard!"

Answer: "If it were really *too* hard, then I couldn't possibly give up this pleasure at all. But of course I can give it up—if I *accept*, without childishly whining about and immensely exaggerating, its difficulty. Apparently it isn't *too* hard for me to whine and moan about it. Only too easy! So I'd better stop *making* it harder than it really is by having a temper tantrum about it. So it's hard! Tough! But it's not *horrible!*"

Disputing: "Even if I never prepare this speech, and even if I find that other people easily and quickly prepare their speeches, how does that wrong behavior of mine, procrastination, make me a thoroughly *incompetent person?*"

Answer: It doesn't, of course. It makes me a person who is not acting competently, right now, in this particular way; and who still has the ability—if I push myself!—to act more competently in the future. If I really were a thoroughly incompetent person, I could do practically nothing well. And that of course is quite false: since I do many things with no trouble at all. So I'd better focus on this incompetent *act*, and not on my 'inadequate personhood.' Yes, I'm still fallible, and will most probably always be. Now how do I stop this procrastinating and make myself *less* fallible? Once again: by prodding—yes, prodding! myself."

Disputing: "Even though I keep spending money on things I really do not need in order to get short-term pleasure that I foolishly think that I do need, how does that indicate that I'll *never* change and will *always* be a stupid spendthrift?"

Answer: It doesn't! No matter how many times I idiotically over-spend, I can most likely change and stop it now and in the future. If my past mistakes proved that I will *never* be able to undo them, I could never have learned the multiplication table! They only prove that I easily and often fail—as just about all humans do. But not *always*! And not that I'm doomed to *never* succeed!"

Disputing: "Let me acknowledge that I have fallen back several times from doing my RET homework, and instead have taken the easier and instantly more gratifying path of not working at changing myself. Where is it written that this makes things *hopeless* and that I *can't* stop indulging in easy things? How does this prove that I might as well give in to my natural tendencies to take things easily and that I should forget about changing myself?"

Answer: "It doesn't! Just because I have natural tendencies to take things easily, and just because I therefore keep falling back from doing my RET homework, I'd better work harder to keep doing and doing this homework, until I acquire a 'second nature' and begin to automatically and fairly easily do it. No matter how difficult it is to do something, or to not give in to any of my compulsions, that never proves that it's *hopeless* and that I *can't* change. Even when something is *next* to impossible, it usually can eventually be done. Fortunately, I *made myself* this way, even though I had great help from my heredity and my environment! And that means that, in all probability, with persistent effort I can make myself act another, better way!"

Keep observing and admitting your backsliding at RET or at anything else, and keep noticing how often and how nicely you are addicted to striving for some kind of immediate gratification rather than for long-range gain and happiness. Stubbornly refuse to put yourself down for your low frustration tolerance; and then keep working to eliminate it. With actual addictive, compulsive, and indulgent behaviors, force yourself many times to stop them. And when you later fall back—as you often may—to indulging in them again, force yourself, no matter how hard it is, to give them up, give them up, give them up.

Because virtually all harmful habits that you favor award you some kind of quick pleasure or payoff, use the principles of reward, reinforcement, or what B. F. Skinner calls operant conditioning (and what other psychologists often call contingency management) to help you give them up. When you contingently reinforce yourself, you pick some action or behavior that is very pleasurable, and preferably even *more* pleasurable than the habit you are trying to give up, and you allow yourself this pleasure AFTER you have refused to engage in the habit you are trying to break.

Suppose, for example, you want to stop smoking cigarettes or want to eat no more than 1500 calories a day. You look for some pleasure that you really find most enjoyable and that you tend to engage in every day in the week—such as listening to music, reading the newspaper, masturbating or having some other kind of sex, having social conversations, exercising, or television viewing. You then allow yourself to have this great pleasure only AFTER you have refrained from smoking or AFTER you have stopped before eating 1501 calories. Be very strict about this reinforcement or reward, or it will not work. No excuses! If you have a single cigarette or eat even 50 extra calories, no music, no newspaper reading, no television viewing, or no other reward that you have set for yourself. Right!—none!

Stiff penalties are even better, if you will properly use them. For you obviously feel real pain or discomfort when you are trying to break a bad habit and actively start breaking it. So pick something even MORE uncomfortable and make yourself do that thing whenever you refuse to give up your harmful habit or whenever you temporarily give it up and then foolishly fall back to it again.

Once more, let us suppose you know that smoking cigarettes will definitely harm you but you self-defeatingly keep smoking. Or suppose you keep unhealthfully gaining weight and had better stay with no more than 1500 calories a day; and, instead, you keep getting up to 1800, 2000, or even 2400 calories a day. How do you penalize yourself every time you go over your own set limits of smoking no cigarettes or eating only 1500 calories? Very simply. Set a strong and very painful penalty—such as lighting every cigarette you smoke with a twenty dollar bill. Or talking to a boring and obnoxious acquaintance for at least an hour every time you take a single puff. Or running for two miles (if you hate running) whenever you eat more than 1500 calories. Or eating a half pound of some food you find very distasteful or taking a sniff of some odor that you find utterly repulsive every single time you eat five calories more than 1500.

Using the principles of immediate reinforcement and quick (and inevitable!) penalties on every occasion when you indulge in bad habits or refuse to engage in good habits (like exercising or doing at least an hour's work on a paper you are writing) won't absolutely make you give up your low frustration tolerance and your tendency to foolishly indulge yourself in pernicious behavior. But it will definitely help!

CHAPTER 17

Insight No. 12: If You Backslide, Try, Try Again

As noted in the previous chapter, humans change for the better—then backslide. You, too!

If you use RET to overcome your misery and you never again fall back to it again—great. But never fear. You will sometimes fall back.

Want to bet?

We prepare our clients at the Institute for Rational-Emotive Therapy by giving them the same pamphlet mentioned above, *How to Maintain and Enhance Your Rational-Emotive Gains.* The second part of this pamphlet, "How to Deal With Backsliding," emphasizes RET *Insight No. 12: When you improve your emotional disturbances, it will be a miracle if you never backslide. When you do, back to the RET drawing board. Try, try again!*

The section of our pamphlet that deals with backsliding makes these points:

1. Accept your backsliding as normal—as something that happens to almost everyone who at first improves emotionally. See it as part of your being a fallible human.

Don't damn yourself when some of your old problems return; and don't think that you have to handle them entirely by yourself and that it is wrong or weak for you to seek help from others.

2. When you backslide, look at your self-defeating *behavior* as bad and unfortunate; but work very hard at refusing to put *yourself* down for engaging in this behavior. Use the highly important RET philosophy of refusing to rate *you*, your*self*, or your *being* but of measuring only your *acts*, *deeds*, and *traits*.

You are always a *person who* acts well or badly—and never a *good person* or a *bad person.* No matter how badly you fall back and make yourself upset again, you can always accept yourself *with* this poor behavior—and then keep trying to *change* this behavior.

3. Go back to the ABCs of RET and see what you did to fall back to your old anxiety or depression. At A (Activating Event), you probably experienced some failure or rejection once again. At rB (rational Belief) you probably told yourself that you didn't *like* failing and didn't *want* to be rejected. If you only stayed with these rational Beliefs, you would merely feel sorry, regretful, disappointed, or frustrated.

But when you felt depressed again, you probably then went on to irrational Beliefs (iBs), such as: "I *must* not fail! It's *horrible* when I do!" "I *have to* be accepted, because if I'm not that makes me an *unlovable, worthless person!*" Then, after convincing yourself of these iBs, you felt, at C (emotional Consequence) once again depressed and self-downing.

4. When you find irrational Beliefs with which you are once again disturbing yourself, just as you originally used Disputing (D) to surrender them, do so again—*immediately* and *persistently.* Thus, you can ask yourself, "Why *must* I not fail? Is it really *horrible* if I do?"

And you can answer: "There is *no* reason why I *must* not fail, though I can think of several reasons why it would be highly undesirable. It's not *horrible* if I do fail—only quite *inconvenient.*"

You can also Dispute your other irrational Beliefs by asking yourself, "Where is it written that I *have* to be accepted? How do I become an *unlovable, worthless person* if I am rejected?"

And you can answer: "I never *have to* be accepted, though I would very much *prefer* to be. If I am rejected, that makes me, alas, a *person who* is rejected this time. But it hardly makes me an *unlovable, worthless person* who will always be rejected by anyone for whom I really care."

5. Keep looking for and vigorously Disputing your irrational Beliefs. Keep doing this, over and over, until you build emotional muscle (just as you would build physical muscle by learning how to exercise and then by *continuing* to exercise).

6. Don't fool yourself into believing that if you merely change your language you will always change your thinking. You may

neurotically tell yourself, "I *must* succeed and be approved," and then you may sanely change this to, "I *prefer* to succeed and be approved." Underneath, however, you may still believe, "But I really *have to* do well and truly *must* be loved."

Before you stop your Disputing and before you are satisfied with your rational answers, keep on working until you are *really* convinced of these rational answers and until your anxiety, depression, and rage truly decline. Then do the same thing many, many times—until your new Effective Philosophy (E) becomes firm. It almost always will, if you keep reworking and repeating it.

If you convince yourself lightly (or "intellectually") of your new Effective Philosophy, it will tend to get through to you lightly— and briefly. Think it through very *strongly* and *vigorously*, and do so many times.

Thus, you can *powerfully* convince yourself, until you really *feel* it: "I do not *need* what I *want*! I never *have to* succeed, no matter how greatly I *wish to* do so!" "I *can* stand being rejected by someone I care for. It won't *kill* me—and I *still* can lead a happy life!" "*No* person is damnable and worthless—including and especially *me*!"

Tony, a member of my therapy group that included Georgiana (whose case I presented in the previous chapter), saw that she worked so well on overcoming her violent feelings of jealousy that he gave himself a similar homework assignment to help overcome his own backsliding. Tony was a forty-six-year-old owner of a retail store, severely anxious and depressed about his business. He desperately *needed*, especially at Christmas time, to do better than last year's sales. When he didn't, he was depressed for the next several months.

Tony was in one of my therapy groups for a year, and every few months we helped him accept uncertainty and stop worrying about his sales. Then he would fall back to renewed feelings of panic. Seeing Georgiana finally maintain her progress, he assigned himself to using the same techniques she used. He concentrated on these points:

1. He at first put himself down greatly for making himself panicked again about his store. But he worked at seeing that his backsliding only showed that he was a normal—though *not* a healthy—fallible human. He shamelessly talked about his renewed anxiety in group and acknowledged it to his family and friends.

2. He was able to see *it*, his backsliding, as bad but not view *himself* as a weak person for letting himself backslide. This *self*-acceptance enabled him to go back to working at getting over *it*.

3. Tony saw, once again, that, when his panic returned, he mainly held the irrational Belief (iB), "I *must* have good sales this year! It would be *horrible* if they fell off. I *couldn't bear* the hardships that would ensue!"

4. He forcefully and persistently asked himself, "Where is it written that I *must* have better sales this year?" Answer: "Only in my nutty head! I don't *have to*, though that would be lovely."

And: "In what way would it be *horrible* if sales fell off?" Answer: "In no way! It would only be damned frustrating. But not the end of my life!"

And: "Could I *really* not bear the hardships of a poor sales year?" Answer: "Obviously I could! I won't go out of business. My family won't starve. And I can work to make things better next year."

5. Tony kept actively and vigorously Disputing his irrational Beliefs until he found it easy to do so and until he regularly arrived at E, his Effective New Philosophies.

6. When he answered himself, at E, "Too bad. If I do poorly at sales, so I do poorly!" he stopped to inquire: "Do I *really* accept that 'too bad' or do I still really think 'It's awful'?" He answered: "Yes, dammit, whether I accept it or not, it *is* too bad. *Not* awful! *Not* unbearable! Just *too damned bad!*"

7. He strongly told himself, many times, "I never *need* good sales. I *can* live and be happy if I don't do better than last year. Loss of income is *never* a holy horror!"

By working at these assignments many times, Tony reached a point where he only occasionally fell back to a state of panic. Fortunately—if we may call it that—he did have one of the worst Christmas seasons he ever had at his store. And although he was disappointed and sorry, he was rarely anxious and never depressed about it. As he reported to his therapy group:

"I lost a hell of a lot of sales and money this Christmas. But I gained a hell of a lot of *me* —of control over my anxiety. That's worth much more than money." The group agreed.

Tony went on to work on other problems—especially his decreased sex drive. His poor retail business, for the first time in years, was easy to accept.

Following the above RET plan, you can stop your own backsliding and can regain any progress that you have made and temporarily lost. If you keep working to do so!

RET Exercise No. 17

Use rational emotive imagery (REI) to get over any emotional upsetness that you may have about falling back to a previous level of disturbance; or use it for almost any other problem of anxiety, depression, or rage that you may have.

In using rational emotive imagery, you first imagine one of the very worst things that might happen to you: for example, you worked very hard to overcome your fear of public speaking or to overcome your addiction to cigarettes, and now you have fallen back again, and in fact have a worse fear than you ever had or are smoking even more cigarettes a day than you ever did before in your life.

You let yourself feel very anxious, depressed, or self-hating about how you have just fallen back after previously working hard and effectively using RET to overcome your fear or your addiction. Let us suppose that as you vividly imagine this worst possible thing happening, you feel exceptionally ashamed, guilty, and self-downing about your allowing yourself to fall back. Get fully in touch, now, with your disturbed feeling and let yourself fully—yes, fully!—experience it for a brief period of time. Don't avoid your feeling of guilt or self-downing. On the contrary, face it and make yourself truly *feel* it.

When you have actually felt, really felt, this disturbed emotion for a while, push yourself—yes, *push* yourself—to change this feeling in your gut, so that instead you *only* experience an appropriate (but still strong) feeling. Thus, make yourself feel keenly disappointed, regretful, annoyed, or irritated with your behavior (for you *have* done a wrong self-defeating thing by letting yourself fall back to your original fear or addiction) but get rid of, actually change your inappropriate feeling of shame, guilt, depression, or self-downing.

As I point out in a pamphlet on rational emotive imagery (REI) that is published by the Institute for Rational-Emotive Therapy in New York (and that is included in the final chapter of *A New Guide to Rational Living*), don't think that you can't do this, can't change your feeling—for you invariably can. Don't forget that *you* —not the Man in the Moon!—created your upsetness in the first place; so *you* —yes, *you* —can always change it in the second place. You can, at almost any time you work at doing so, get in touch with your gut-level feelings and push yourself to change them so that you experience different feelings. You definitely have the ability to do this. So try, concentrate—and do it!

When you have let yourself, pushed yourself *only* to feel sorry, regretful, disappointed, or irritated (instead of ashamed, guilty, depressed, and self-downing) look at what you have done in your head to *make yourself* have these new, appropriate (though still negative) feelings. You will see, if you observe yourself clearly, that you have in some manner changed your Belief System (or irrational Beliefs or Bullshit) at B, and have thereby changed your emotional Consequences, at C, so that you now feel appropriate instead of inappropriate emotions. Become fully aware of the rational Beliefs (rBs) that you have used to create your new appropriate emotional Consequences (Cs) regarding the unpleasant Activating Experience (A) that you have imagined or fantasized.

Thus, in this particular case, A was the observation that you have fallen back to your old phobia or addiction. At iB, you told yourself something like, "I should not have fallen back! How awful and shameful to fall back! I'm a pretty incompetent person to let myself do a foolish thing like that!" Then you felt depressed, guilty, self-hating. Now, if you do the rational emotive imagery correctly, you have changed to a new set of rBs (rational Beliefs), such as: "It was most unfortunate and unpleasant that I fell back but that is the nature of humans, including myself, to take two steps forward and one step backward. And sometimes two or three steps backward! I'm hardly an incompetent person to let myself do a foolish thing like that, but a fairly competent person who sometimes acts incompetently. And that is my nature, too!—to at times act foolishly. What a pain in the butt! But I can do better than that, I am sure, in the future; and get right back to the progress that I formerly made. Okay: back to the drawing board!"

Observe and understand that these new, rational Beliefs are the ones that made you change your feelings; and practice changing your disturbed feelings again and again, by repeating this kind of rational Belief. If your upsetting feelings do not change as you attempt to feel more appropriately, keep fantasizing the same unpleasant experiences or events and keep working on your gut until you *do* change your feelings to appropriate ones. Never forget: *You* create and control your feelings. Therefore, *you* can invariably change them.

Once you succeed in feeling sorry, regretful, disappointed, irritated, and frustrated rather than anxious, depressed, guilty, and self-downing about your falling back (or about any of your other disruptive emotions and behaviors), and once you see exactly what Beliefs you have changed in your head to make yourself feel badly but not emotionally upset, keep repeating this process. Make yourself feel really disturbed. Then make yourself feel displeased but not disturbed. Then see exactly what you did in your head to change your feelings. Then practice doing this same kind of thing, over and over again. Keep practicing, until you can easily, after you imagine highly unfortunate experiences (such as falling back in your self-therapy after you have previously made some progress) at point A, feel upset at point C, change your feelings at point C to those of disappointment and sorrow but not upsetness, and see what you keep doing at point B to change your Belief system that creates and maintains your feelings. If you keep practicing this kind of rational emotive imagery (REI) at least once (and preferably two or three times) every day for the next few weeks, you will tend to reach the point where whenever you think of this same kind of unpleasant event, or it actually occurs in your life, you will easily and automatically feel displeased and sorry rather than inappropriately depressed and self-downing.

REI, then, can be done imaginatively before an unfortunate event (like falling back in your progress) occurs. It can also be done at the same time that the event actually occurs. And if you miss doing it when it occurs, it can be done an hour later, or a day or two later. In all cases, you let yourself feel really guilty, ashamed, depressed, or anxious, and then you push yourself to feel disappointed and frustrated but *not* truly upset.

Suppose you promise yourself to do REI at least once a day about your falling back from your RET progress (or about anything else that you upset yourself about) and suppose that you keep postponing it and failing to do it. You can then use reinforcement by rewarding yourself with something you really like to do (such as reading, eating, television viewing, or social contacts with your friends) *after* you have done the rational imagery as often as you have promised yourself to do it; and you can penalize yourself with something you really dislike (such as eating something obnoxious, contributing to a cause you hate, burning a twenty dollar bill, or getting up a half hour earlier in the morning) when you have *not* done REI as you have promised yourself to do it. You may do REI without this kind of reinforcement or penalizing, but if you have trouble doing it this way, then you may help yourself by resorting to reinforcement methods. Similarly, if you procrastinate on any other important task, you can reward yourself *after* you do it and penalize yourself when you don't. This system won't absolutely *make* you do what you want to do. But it will often help!

CHAPTER 18

Insight No. 13: You Can Extend Your Refusal to Make Yourself Miserable

RET gives you two kinds of solutions to your emotional problems: (1) Immediate, limited, and short-lived answers; and (2) Long-lived, extended, and elegant answers. Even its less elegant and short-range answers are pretty good: For they show you how to quickly rid yourself of feelings of anxiety, depression, self-hatred, hostility, and self-pity. And how to reduce your lethargy, incompetence, procrastination, phobias, compulsions, and addictions.

But RET's extended and long-lasting solutions are better. For they show you—

How to maintain your improvement.

How to rarely upset yourself again in the same way.

How to quickly recover when you fall back.

How to generalize from your original disturbance to other upsets that you may experience.

How to overcome—and maintain your victory over—any kind of neurotic problem for the rest of your life.

How to stubbornly refuse to make yourself miserable over anything—yes, anything.

For RET insists that your neurotic problems stem from three basic kinds of godlike, *must*urbatory thinking, and that if you surrender your unrealistic and unscientific dogmas, you can see that all your emotional problems stem from similar irrational Beliefs. You can then extend your RET answers to your other destructive behaviors. RET thereby gives you specific *and* general solutions to emotional pain.

This brings us to *Insight No. 13: Once you understand the basic irrational Beliefs (iBs) you create to upset yourself, you can use this understanding to explore, attack, and surrender your other present and future emotional problems.*

How do you broaden your use of RET from solving one set of emotional problems to reducing your other miseries? Here are some ways to extend your results to other possible troubles:

1. Show yourself that your present upsetness and the ways in which you create it are not unique. Admit that virtually all your emotional problems are created by your own irrational Beliefs (iBs). Therefore—fortunately!—you can *un*create these iBs by firmly and steadily disputing and acting against them.

2. Once again, recognize that you mainly use these irrational Beliefs (iBs) to disturb yourself:

(a) "I *must* do well and *have to* be approved by people whom I find important." This iB makes you feel anxious, depressed, and self-hating; and leads you to avoid doing things at which you may fail and to run away from relationships that may not turn out well.

(b) "Other people *must* treat me fairly and nicely!" This iB makes you feel angry, furious, violent, and over-rebellious.

(c) "The conditions under which I live *must* be comfortable and free from major hassles!" This iB creates feelings of low frustration tolerance and self-pity; and sometimes those of anger and depression. It also leads to procrastination, compulsions, and addictions.

3. Recognize that when you employ these three dogmatic *musts* you easily derive several other irrational conclusions from them. Such as:

(a) "Because I am not doing as well as I *must*, I am an incompetent, worthless person!" (Self-downing)

(b) "Since I am not being approved by important people, as I *have to be,* it's *awful* and *terrible*! It's the end of the world!" (Awfulizing; terribleizing; catastrophizing)

(c) "Because others are not treating me as fairly and as nicely as they *absolutely should* treat me, they are *utterly rotten people* and deserve to be damned!" (Damnation)

(d) "Since the conditions under which I live are not as comfortable as they *should be,* and since my life has several major hassles, as it *must* not have, I *can't stand* it! My existence is a horror!" (Can't-stand-it-itis)

(e) "Because I have failed as I *ought* not and have been rejected as I *absolutely should not* have been, I'll *always* fail and *never* get accepted as I *must* be! My life will be hopeless and joyless forever!" (Overgeneralizing; hopelessness)

4. Work at seeing that these irrational Beliefs *often* and *generally* upset you. See that you bring them to *many* different kinds of undesirable situations.

Realize that in just about all cases where you feel anxious and depressed and where you act foolishly you are consciously or unconsciously sneaking in one or more of these iBs. Consequently, if you reject them in one area and are still disturbed about something else, you can use the same RET principles to discover your irrational Beliefs in the new area and to eliminate them there.

5. Keep showing yourself that it is almost impossible to disturb yourself in *any* way if you abandon your rigid, dogmatic *shoulds,* *oughts,* and *musts* and if you replace them with flexible (though still strong) *desires* and *preferences.*

6. Continue to acknowledge that you can change your irrational Beliefs (iBs) by powerfully using the scientific method. With scientific thinking, you can show yourself that your irrational Beliefs are only assumptions—not facts. You can logically and realistically Dispute them in many ways, such as these:

(a) You can show yourself that your iBs are self-defeating— that they interfere with your goals and your happiness. For if you rigidly convince yourself, "I *must* succeed at important tasks and *have to* be approved by all the important people I meet," you will at times fail and be disapproved—and thereby make yourself feel anxious and depressed instead of sorry and frustrated.

(b) Your irrational Beliefs do not conform to reality—and especially do not conform to the fact that humans are imperfect and fallible.

If you always *had* to succeed, if the universe commanded that you *must* do so, you obviously *would* always succeed. And of course you often don't!

If you invariably *had* to be approved by others, you could never be disappointed. But clearly you frequently are!

The universe plainly does *not* always give you everything you demand. So although your desires are often realistic, your god-like commands definitely are not!

(c) Your irrational Beliefs do not follow from your rational premises or assumptions and are therefore illogical and absurd. "I strongly *want* to succeed" doesn't lead to "Therefore I *must!*" No matter how desirable justice is, it never, therefore, *has to* exist.

Although the scientific method is not infallible or sacred, it helps you discover which of your beliefs are irrational and self-defeating and how to use facts and logical thinking to give them up. If you think scientifically, you will avoid dogma and keep your hypotheses about yourself, about other people, and about the world always open to change.

7. Try to establish some main goals and purposes in life—goals that you would *like* very much to reach but that you never *absolutely must* attain. Keep checking to see how you are coming along with these goals. At times revise them. See how you feel when you achieve them. You don't *have to* have long-range goals. But they help!

8. If you get bogged down and begin to lead a life that seems miserable or dull, review the points made here and work at using them. There's rarely any gain without pain!

Many of my clients, alas, refuse to extend their use of RET, even though it helped them to quickly—sometimes "miraculously"— overcome the problem that drove them to therapy. Because, often, they have low frustration tolerance (LFT) and refuse to march on to extended and elegant RET solutions.

Not so Malvina. When she first came to RET, she was a highly attractive nineteen-year-old student, majoring in history. Although bright and talented (especially in music), she was a social basket case. She was too shy to date. She had no close female friends. She considered herself plain and not too intelligent. She was severely depressed and often thought about suicide. She had no real career goals. She hated her parents—both of whom were severely depressed, too—and blamed them for her troubles.

Three years of psychoanalysis had done little for Malvina but only helped her become more hostile toward her family and dependent on her analyst. Although her friends did their best to get her away from the analyst, nothing worked until he had a heart attack, retired, and moved to Florida. She tried to keep in touch with him by phone, but he finally refused her calls. The only reason she agreed to see me was that at that time I was his exact age, fifty-one, and looked somewhat like him.

For many months I got nowhere with Malvina, as I tried to show her that her own crooked, self-damning thoughts—and not the "horrible teachings" of her parents—mainly created her feelings of depression. At first, she wouldn't accept these RET techniques.

I kept showing her that she had several strong irrational Beliefs—especially, "I *must* always be exceptionally beautiful, bright, and lovable and I'm worthless when I fall short of this!" She finally admitted, "I guess you're right. I am idiotically depressing myself." But instead of working to give this up, she immediately started berating herself "for being so stupidly irrational," and she became, if possible, more depressed.

On several occasions, Malvina talked so much about suicide that I encouraged her to go for anti-depressants and to consider entering a hospital. She refused to consider medication, but the threat of being hospitalized encouraged her to work at accepting and using RET.

First, Malvina stopped blaming herself for being so disturbed. She worked hard to stop upsetting herself *about* being upset; and she began to accept herself *with* her depression.

Although when Malvina stopped damning herself for being disturbed she became one of the most *relaxed* depressives I have ever seen, she still often blamed herself for her "plainness" (she had "too large" a nose), for her "stupidity" (she only achieved Bs instead of As at math), and for her lack of career goals. But—because she now really saw the ABCs of RET and saw how Disputing helped her give up the irrational Belief that she *must* not be depressed—she decided to work at overcoming *all* her self-damning.

She did.

Malvina first accepted herself with her "plainness"—and then saw that she was fairly attractive. She stopped blaming herself for her "stupidity"—and then realized she was intelligent. She convinced herself that it was *too bad* but not *awful*, that she had no career vocational goals—and then started planning to get some.

Although she now realized she was attractive and bright, Malvina used rational emotive imagery to vividly imagine herself becoming *really* ugly and stupid. She then made herself feel only sorry and regretful, instead of depressed, because she told herself that even under these grim conditions, she still could—and *would* —accept herself and strive to lead a fairly happy existence.

After several months of refusing to belittle herself, Malvina for the first time in her life felt completely undepressed. Better yet, she realized that she could soon reduce her other feelings of anxiety and shame by strongly counterattacking all her self-putdowns.

To make her gains more solid, Malvina also tackled her awfulizing and concluded, "It's not *awful* —only *annoying* —that I am not very good in math!" She worked against her can't-stand-it-itis, until she convinced herself, "I *can* bear my large nose though I'll never like it." And she fought stoutly against her ideas of hopelessness and replaced them with, "Although I haven't come up with a suitable career yet, there's no reason why I *never* will. It's hard to find something I really will like. But it's hardly hopeless!"

In addition to using scientific thinking and firmly attacking her dogmatic *musts*, Malvina began helping her friends see and Dispute their own irrational Beliefs. She did so well in this respect that she finally found her career. She went for graduate work in clinical psychology and for the last fifteen years has been an excellent rational-emotive therapist. She enjoys her work immensely. She has several close friends. After a few years of comfortable dating, she successfully married and is the happy (and rational!) mother of a nine-year-old daughter.

Is Malvina now happy *because* she is a successful psychologist, wife, mother, and friend? Yes. But she insists, when I see her at professional meetings, that she would be undepressed and unanxious even if she had failed in these respects. I believe her, because she has worked exceptionally hard at extending the ABCs and DEs of RET to *any* feelings of anxiety and depression she may experience. So she has achieved the elegant rational-emotive solution.

You, once you use RET to overcome any of your main problems, may not have to work as hard as Malvina to generalize and extend it to your other emotional difficulties. But if you do, you do! If you follow RET's *Insight No. 13*, you can use the rational ideas that helped you overcome one problem to show yourself how you can conquer other neurotic difficulties. Once again—if you *work* at doing so!

Exercise No. 18

Imagine that you have overcome one of your greatest anxieties—such as your fear of writing, or public speaking, or sexual rejections, or doing poorly at work. You are feeling fine about this, but now you see that you have developed a new fear—say, talking to people at parties or other social gatherings.

· First, see if you feel really upset—downed or depressed—about this new anxiety. If you do, use rational emotive imagery to make yourself feel *only* disappointed with your behavior, but not horrified about you, the person who has fallen back. To change your inappropriate feeling, tell yourself rational self-statements, such as: "I don't like my foolishly falling back and creating a new irrational fear, but that doesn't make me a *total* fool!" Or: "Too bad I created another silly anxiety, but I'm still fallible in that respect and I can work at becoming somewhat less fallible but never perfect."

Once you really begin to accept *you* in spite of your new irrational *behavior*, look for the things in common between the irrational Beliefs (iBs) creating your new anxiety and those that you worked on to give up your old anxiety. For example, suppose you previously feared doing poorly at work and you now fear socializing at parties.

Your previous iB may have been: "I must impress my fellow workers." Your new iB may be· "I must impress the people I meet at social gatherings."

Again, your old iB may have been, "My fellow workers must not put me down. If they do and I don't tell them off, I'm a real schnook and a wimp!" Your new iB may be, "People at social gatherings must not scorn me and laugh at me. If they do and I don't very wittily get back at them, I'm a schnook and an idiot!"

When you discover the common irrational Beliefs that led to the original anxiety you overcame and you see how they are repeated to create your new set of anxieties, use the same kind of Disputing and the same kind of other RET techniques that you successfully used to overcome your previous irrational fears and persist at them until you also can use them to overcome your new fears.

Since there are only a few basic iBs that lead to anxiety, depression, guilt, hostility, and self-downing, when you see that you have a new disturbed feeling, or a variation of one of the old ones, assume that you *once again* can find the iBs that you are using to create your new symptoms. And when you do find these iBs— which you will, if you *persist* —use techniques of Disputing and other RET procedures which you found worked well on the old emotional problems. Don't give up! Keep working at it! And almost invariably you will find that similar neurotic symptoms stem from similar iBs. Try generalizing in this respect—and see how well it often works!

The same thing goes for your self-defeating behaviors. You may have been compulsively addicted, say, to overeating and you overcame your addiction by discovering your iBs—such as, "I *need* this delicious food, I *can't stand* being deprived of it!"—and by changing them. Now you may be compulsively addicted to smoking or to caffeine, and you can often find similar *needs* and *I-can't-stand-its* that are making you addicted. If you formerly proved to yourself that you *don't* need delicious food and *can* stand being deprived of it, you can similarly now prove to yourself that you do *not* need smoking or caffeine and definitely *can* stand their loss. Just as you once forced yourself to *uncomfortably* push away the extra food, you can now force yourself to push away the unnecessary cigarettes and coffee. You were uncomfortable but did not die the first time. Nor will you die of discomfort now!

You can also generalize from your successful use of emotive RET techniques. Thus, you may have overcome your guilt about not visiting your in-laws every week by very vigorously telling yourself, "I'm not upsetting them by refusing to see them as often as they demand. *They* are responsible for their own upsetness. Too bad! If they hate me, they hate me! I can live *with* that. At worst, I'm rotten to my in-laws but that doesn't make me a *rotten person!*" To get over guilt or shame about other things—such as disclosing one of your weaknesses to people or not being the greatest parent who ever lived—you can generalize from your past RET success and use a similar emotive method to overcome the new aspect of your self-downing.

Whenever, then, you have used RET to reduce one aspect of your disturbance, ask yourself how you can use it to overcome other aspects. And *practice* using this RET technique again and again in somewhat similar circumstances until it becomes second nature for you to employ it in various areas of your disturbance.

CHAPTER 19

Insight No. 14: Yes, You Can Stubbornly Refuse to Make Yourself Severely Anxious or Depressed About Anything

Suppose the very worst—yes, the *worst*—happens, can you still stubbornly refuse to make yourself severely anxious or depressed about anything?

Yes. Definitely, yes.

Don't forget that you are a *creative* human. If you even *partly* use your creativity, you can be unmiserable—and at times even happy—under some of the most unfortunate conditions.

Let me illustrate with an extreme case, which was told to me years ago by a famous American musician. He knew an elderly retired couple who had lost their only child, a bright and very attractive boy, when he died of pneumonia at the age of six. They took this loss very well, and continued to do so even after they tried unsuccessfully to have another child.

For many years after their son's death, people would say to them, "Isn't it sad that you lost such a charming child? Imagine how nice it would be if he were still alive. He would be such a comfort to you. He'd probably be married by now and you'd have grandchildren to lighten your life as you grow older. Of course, you are very sad about such a great loss!"

"Oh, no," this couple would immediately respond. "We don't feel sad at all when we think about Marvie and his death."

"You don't?" would come the astonished query.

"No, of course not. He was such a fine boy and led such a good life while he was here. And now that he's gone, we are sure that God is taking the best of care of him in Heaven, and that he is, and will always be, very happy there. So we are not at all sad about what happened to him."

Both these parents would then genuinely beam and convince everyone, especially themselves, how happy they were in the face of this grim loss.

Cover-up? Defensive denial? I would say, yes. Did this couple repress their underlying feelings of sadness, perhaps even depression? Again, probably yes. So I by no means recommend their refusing to acknowledge their severe loss. In fact, I am highly suspicious of it.

The main point I am making, however, is this: People *can* change their feelings. No matter what happens to them, they *can* creatively decide to feel one way or another about it. And they have quite a range of possible feelings to choose from!

Do you really want to test out this freedom of choice in your own life? All right, let's experiment. Let us imagine some of the worst things that might happen to you—things that you would clearly dislike, and about which you might easily make yourself anxious, depressed, or enraged. I am going to present some of these grim events to you and ask you, if you strongly use the RET insights we have been discussing in this book, how you would rationally cope with them and make yourself feel appropriately sad, displeased, and annoyed but *not* inappropriately panicked and destroyed.

Ready?

Question: Suppose you find, after a long search, a job that is ideal for you and suppose you foolishly come late to work, are lazy, act nastily to your boss, and get fired. What can you rationally and emotionally tell yourself?

RET Answer: You can tell yourself: "Too bad! I certainly behaved poorly this time. But that hardly makes me a stupid or incompetent person. Just someone who needlessly did myself in. Now what can I do to find another job like this one, work hard at it, and please my boss? But even if I never get as good a job again, I am determined to do the best I can, and to be as effective and as happy as I can be with a worse position."

Question: Suppose you have a serious accident and lose an arm or a leg—or even your vision—how can you manage to live with those kinds of handicaps?

RET Answer: Not so well! You certainly would feel greatly deprived and frustrated. But not necessarily depressed! If you tell yourself, "Although my abilities and pleasures are seriously limited, I can still do many interesting and enjoyable things and can find ways to compensate for my disabilities. Instead of focusing dismally on what I can *not* do, I can concentrate on the many interests and pleasures I can *still* have and thereby almost guarantee myself a reasonably happy existence."

Question: Suppose you bought a stock at a low price, felt anxious about how high it might go, and sold it only at a small profit, instead of the large amount you could have made if you had held on to it a while longer. Can you still refuse to make yourself miserable about that?

RET Answer: You damned well can! Even if you stupidly sold at exactly the wrong time and lost money on the stock, while everybody else held on until they made a mint, you could make yourself feel disappointed—but not self-hating—about your loss. You could convince yourself, "If I choose to gamble at anything, I had better acknowledge that it *is* a gamble, and that there is never a certainty of winning. Second, no one buys and sells stocks and always makes maximum gains. Including me! Third, it was good that I made *anything* on the deal. What luck! Fourth, this gives me a chance to see what I am doing to foolishly make myself anxious about this deal, and what I can do in the future to make myself less anxious. Fifth, making a pile of money is good and will make me happi*er*. But I can also be distinctly happy with less money. *If* I stop berating myself for making less!"

Question: Suppose your beloved mate or one of your close friends for whom you really care dies. How can you rationally deal with that great loss?

RET Answer: By steadfastly *accepting*, without at all *liking*, what you can't change. Firmly tell yourself: "Death, so far, is inevitable for all of us. Nor could I have prevented this death. I shall miss this person considerably and feel truly deprived of companionship and pleasure. But I can still think of the fine times we did have. And I can realize that he or she gave me great joy, though the feeling I had was *my* feeling and I *can* have similar feelings and pleasure with others. What can I *now* do to increase my ability to love and to find suitable partners to care for?"

Question: Suppose you no longer can enjoy the main things you

used to enjoy—such as sports, or work, or romantic love, or sex
Isn't that good reason to feel depressed?

RET Answer: Definitely not! You would then clearly have *less*
satisfaction, *less* pleasure in life. But hardly *none*. Unless you foolishly depress yourself by telling yourself, "I *must* still have these
former enjoyments." Then you *will* ruin your life and enjoy virtually *nothing*. But if you no longer can thrill to sports, work, sex, or
anything else, you can almost certainly, as long as you are truly
alive, find *something* that you really like. What? Seek, experiment
and find out. Just thinking can be enjoyable. Or even television! As
long as you stop convincing yourself that life without *certain* pleasures is *totally* unsatisfying!

Question: Suppose you are in constant physical pain (for example, from advanced cancer), you really don't enjoy anything, and
you are pretty certain that this painful existence will continue until
you die. What can you then do to avoid real misery?

RET Answer: Very little, physically. And emotionally you would
hardly be happy! If I were in that sad condition and had no important goal to keep fulfilling—such as to help my loved ones or to
finish a major project—I might rationally, calmly, decide to pain-
lessly kill myself. For though I definitely find life good, it is hardly
sacred, and is not good under *all* conditions. So if my pain blocked
all satisfactions, I would see little sense in living. But I wouldn't
desperately depart. I would feel thankful for the life I had had, feel
sorry that it was now so painful, and feel glad that I could think of
some quick way of ending it. My other choice might well be to focus on some important thing I could do—such as finish a major
book I was writing—and bear my pain until I at least finished this
project. In either case, I would use rational thinking to show myself that even the "worst" conditions are not "horrible."

Question: Suppose you find a most unusual love partner with
whom you are very happy and you then act so meanly with this
person that he or she leaves you and goes off with someone else.
How can you stubbornly refuse to make yourself depressed?

RET Answer: By doing exactly that: stubbornly refusing to make
yourself depressed. You can tell yourself, "That was mean
behavior—but that never makes me a mean and rotten *person*! I'd
better admit that I made myself unlovable this time and ruined a
fine relationship. But again, this foolish *conduct* doesn't by any
means make me a totally unlovable *individual*. If I recognize my

great loss and truly regret it, I can work hard at being less mean and more caring in the future and do my best to win back my partner's love. Or, if that is impossible, I can push myself to look for another mate, act much better next time, and work to establish a fine relationship."

Question: Suppose that you know for sure that you're soon to die in an atomic holocaust and that, in fact, the whole human race will perish with you and completely die out. How would you feel, and what would you do?

RET Answer: Let me, once again, give my own answer. For a few minutes, I would make myself feel damned sad and frustrated. "What fools these mortals be! How foolish and unnecessary!" I would tell myself. "But if that's the way humans are, that's the way they are! Tough!" Then I would try my best to have a damned good time—eating, loving, and having sex while listening to great music!—during the last minutes or days of my one and only earthly existence.

What do all these questions and answers show? That much of your discomfort, pain, failure, rejection, and loss cannot be avoided or eliminated. Life, as we say in RET, is frequently spelled H-A-S-S-L-E. A good deal of it, with thought and effort, you can greatly improve. Not all! Not completely!

Tough. But not awful, not horrible, not terrible. Just tough.

Now—how are you going to arrange for greater *enjoyment*?

Notes

CHAPTER 1
1. The main other self-help RET books that I have published, which partially but not completely cover some of the material in the present book, include: Ellis, 1972a, 1972b, 1976a, 1977, 1979; Ellis & Becker, 1982; Ellis & Harper, 1961, 1975; Ellis & Knaus, 1977; Ellis, Wolfe & Moseley, 1966.

CHAPTER 2
1. Bandura, 1977; Beck, 1976; Bernard, 1986; Ellis, 1957, 1962, 1971, 1973, 1977a; Ellis & Abrahms, 1978; Ellis & Bernard, 1983, 1985; Ellis & Dryden, 1987; Ellis & Grieger, 1986; Ellis & Harper, 1961, 1975; Ellis & Whiteley, 1979; Goldfried & Davison, 1976; Glasser, 1965; Guidano & Liotti, 1983; Mahoney, 1974; Mahoney & Freeman, 1985; Martin, 1987; Meichenbaum, 1977; Raimy, 1976; Wolfe & Brand, 1977.
2. Same references as in No 1, Chapter 2.
3. Ellis, 1962, 1973; 1977a, 1985a, 1985b, 1987a, 1987b; Horney, 1945.
4. DiGiuseppe, Miller & Trexler, 1979; Ellis, 1979; Engels & Diekstra, 1987 Haaga & Davison, in press; McGovern & Silverman, 1984; Miller & Berman, 1983; Smith & Glass, 1977.

CHAPTER 3
1. Bartley, 1962; Popper, 1962; Russell, 1965.

CHAPTER 5
1. Freud, 1965.
2. Ellis, 1962, 1968.

CHAPTER 6
1. Beck, 1976; Lazarus, 1966; Lazarus & Folkman, 1984; Meichenbaum, 1977; Wolpe, 1984.

CHAPTER 8
1. Horney, 1945.
2. Ellis, 1976b.
3. Ellis, 1958.
4. See reference in Note 4, Chapter 2.
5. Baisden, 1980; Beck, 1967, 1976; Smith, in press.

CHAPTER 9
1. Bard, 1980; Bernard, 1986; Ellis, 1957, 1962, 1971, 1973, 1985a; Ellis & Dryden, 1987; Ellis & Grieger, 1986; Ellis & Whiteley, 1979; Grieger & Boyd, 1980; Grieger & Grieger, 1982; Martin, 1987; Maultsby, 1984; Walen, DiGiuseppe & Wessler, 1980; Wessler & Wessler, 1980; Wolfe & Brand, 1977.

CHAPTER 11

1. Bernard, 1986; Ellis, 1962, 1985a, 1987a; Ellis & Becker, 1982; Ellis & Bernard, 1985; Ellis & Dryden, 1987; Ellis & Harper, 1975.

CHAPTER 12

1. Ellis, 1962, 1971, 1976a, 1979a; Ellis & Abrahms, 1978; Ellis & Becker, 1982; Ellis & Dryden, 1987; Ellis & Knaus, 1977.

CHAPTER 13

1. Ellis, 1958, 1962, 1973, 1985a; Ellis & Dryden, 1987; Ellis & Grieger, 1986; Ellis & Whiteley, 1979.
2. Ellis, 1962, 1985a, 1987a; Ellis & Abrahms, 1978; Ellis & Becker, 1982; Ellis & Dryden, 1987; Ellis & Whiteley, 1979.
3. Ellis, 1954.
4. Jones, 1924a, 1924b; Watson & Rayner, 1920.
5. Ellis, 1954, 1962.

CHAPTER 14

1. Ellis, 1962.
2. Adler, 1927, 1964; Coué, 1923; Ellenberger, 1970; Dubois, 1907.
3. Ellis, 1979-80; 1985a; Ellis & Dryden, 1987.
4. Ellis, 1977b, 1977c, 1987c.

CHAPTER 15

1. Abelson, 1963; Zajonc, 1980.
2. Ellis, 1977, 1985a, 1987a, 1987b; Ellis & Harper, 1975; Ellis & Dryden, 1987.

CHAPTER 16

1. Ellis, 1984.
2. Ellis, 1973; Ellis & Becker, 1982; Ellis & Harper, 1975; Ellis & Knaus, 1977a; Hauck, 1973; Young, 1974.

References

Included in the following list of references are items preceded by an asterisk (*). These are materials in the area of rational-emotive therapy (RET), many of which are published or distributed by the Institute for Rational-Emotive Therapy, 45 East 65th Street, New York, New York 10021-6593, (212) 535-0822. The Institute will continue to make available these and other materials on rational-emotive therapy, as well as to present talks, seminars, workshops, and other presentations in the area of human growth and rational living. If you are interested, send for its current catalogue of publications, events, recordings, and other materials.

Abelson, R. P. (1963). Computer stimulation of "hot" cognition. In S. S. Tompkins & S. Messick (Eds.), *Computer stimulation of personality.* New York: Wiley.

Adler, A. (1927). *Understanding human nature.* New York: Greenberg.

Adler, A. (1929). *The science of living.* New York: Greenberg.

Adler, A. (1931). *What life should mean to you.* New York: Blue Ribbon Books.

Adler, A. (1964). *Superiority and social interest.* (Ed.) by H. L. Ansbacher & R. R. Ansbacher. Evanston, IL: Northwestern University Press.

Adler, A. (1964). *Social interest: A challenge to mankind.* New York: Capricorn.

*Alberti, R. E., & Emmons, M. L. (1986). *Your perfect right.* 5th Ed. San Luis Obispo, CA: Impact.

Anderson, C. (1966). Depression and suicide reassessed. *Rational Living,* 1(2), 31–36.

Ansbacher, H. L., & Ansbacher, R. (1956). *The individual psychology of Alfred Adler.* New York: Basic Books.

*Ard, B. N., Jr., & Ard, C. (Eds.) (1969). *Handbook of marriage counseling.* Palo Alto, CA: Science and Behavior Books.

*Baisden, H. E. (1980). *Irrational beliefs: A construct validation study.* Unpublished doctoral dissertation. University of Minnesota.

Bandura, A. (1977). *Social learning theory.* Englewood Cliffs, NJ: Prentice-Hall.

*Bard, J. (1980). *Rational-emotive therapy in practice.* Champaign, IL: Research Press.

184   *References*

*Barrish, H. H., & Barrish, I. J. (1985). *Managing parental anger: The coping parent series*. Kansas: Overland Press.

Bartley, W. W. (1962). *The retreat to commitment*. New York: Knopf.

Beck, A. T. (1967). *Depression*. New York: Hoeber-Harper.

Beck, A. T. (1976). *Cognitive therapy and the emotional disorders*. New York: International Universities Press.

Beck, A. T., & Emery, G. (1985). *Anxiety disorders and phobias*. New York: Basic Books.

Beck, A. T., Rush, A. J., Shaw, B. F. & Emery, G. (1979). *Cognitive therapy of depression*. New York: Guilford.

*Bernard, M. E., & DiGiuseppe, R. (Eds.) (in press). *Inside rational-emotive therapy*. Orlando, FL: Academic Press.

*Bernard, M. E., & Joyce, M. R. (1984). *Rational-emotive therapy with children and adolescents*. New York: Wiley.

*Bernard, M. E. (1986). *Staying alive in an irrational world: Albert Ellis and rational-emotive therapy*. South Melbourne, Australia: Carlson/ Macmillan.

Bone, H. (1968). Two proposed alternatives to psychoanalytic interpretation. In E. Hammer (Ed.), *Use of interpretation in treatment* (pp. 169–196). New York: Grune and Stratton.

Burns, D. D. (1980). *Feeling good: The new mood therapy*. New York: Morrow.

Corey, G. (1986). *Theory and practice of counseling and psychotherapy*. 3rd ed. Monterey, CA: Brooks/Cole.

Corey, G. (1986). *Case approach to counseling and psychotherapy*. 2nd ed. Monterey, CA: Brooks/Cole.

Coué, E. (1923). *My method*. New York: Doubleday, Page.

*Crawford, T., & Ellis, A. (in press). A dictionary of rational-emotive feelings and behaviors. *Journal of Rational-Emotive and Cognitive-Behavioral Therapy*.

Danysh, J. (1974). *Stop without quitting*. San Francisco: International Society for General Semantics.

*DiGiuseppe, R. (1975). *A developmental study of the efficacy of rational-emotive education*. Ph.D. thesis, Hofstra University.

*DiGiuseppe, R. (1986). The implication of the philosophy of science for rational-emotive theory and therapy. *Psychotherapy, 23*, 634–639.

*DiGiuseppe, R. A., Miller, N. J., & Trexler, L. D. (1979). A review of rational-emotive psychotherapy outcome studies. In A. Ellis & J. M. Whiteley (Eds.), *Theoretical and empirical foundations of rational-emotive therapy* (pp. 218–235) Monterey, CA: Brooks/Cole.

*DiMattia, D. J. (Producer). (1987). *Mind over myths: Handling difficult situations in the workplace*. New York: Institute for Rational-Emotive Therapy.

Dryden, W. (1984). *Rational-emotive therapy: Fundamentals and innovations.* Beckenham, Kent: Croom-Helm.

*Dryden, W. (1984). Rational-emotive therapy. In W. Dryden (Ed.), *Individual therapy in Britain* (pp. 235–263). London: Harper & Row.

*Dryden, W., Backx, W., & Ellis, A. (1987). Problems in living: The Friday night workshop. In W. Dryden, *Current issues in rational-emotive therapy* (pp. 154–170). London and New York: Croom Helm.

*Dryden, W. & Ellis, A. (1986). Rational-emotive therapy (RET). In W. Dryden & W. Golden (Eds.), *Cognitive-behavioural approaches to psychotherapy* (pp. 129–168). London: Harper & Row.

*Dryden, W. & Golden, W. L. (1986). *Cognitive-behavioural approaches to psychotherapy.* London: Harper & Row.

*Dryden, W. & Trower, P. (Eds.). (1986). *Rational-emotive therapy: Recent developments in theory and practice.* Bristol, England: Institute for RET (UK).

Dubois, P. (1907). *The psychic treatment of nervous disorders.* New York: Funk & Wagnalls.

Ellenberger, H. F. (1970). *The discovery of the unconscious.* New York: Basic Books.

Ellis, A. (1951). *The folklore of sex.* New York: Charles Boni. Rev. ed.: New York: Grove Press, 1961.

*Ellis, A. (1954). *The American sexual tragedy.* New York: Twayne and Grove Press. Revised edition, New York: Lyle Stuart and Grove Press, 1962.

*Ellis, A. (1957). *How to live with a neurotic: At home and at work.* New York: Crown. Revised edition, Hollywood, CA: Wilshire Books, 1975.

*Ellis, A. (1958). Rational psychotherapy. *Journal of General Psychology,* 59, 35–49. Reprinted: New York: Institute for Rational-Emotive Therapy.

*Ellis, A. (1958). *Sex without guilt.* New York: Lyle Stuart. Rev. ed., New York: Lyle Stuart, 1965.

*Ellis, A. (1960). *The art and science of love.* Secaucus, NJ: Lyle Stuart.

*Ellis, A. (1962). *Reason and emotion in psychotherapy.* Secaucus, NJ: Lyle Stuart.

*Ellis, A. (1963). *The intelligent woman's guide to manhunting.* New York: Lyle Stuart. Rev. ed., *The intelligent woman's guide to dating and mating.* Secaucus, NJ: Lyle Stuart, 1979.

*Ellis, A. (1965). *Suppressed: Seven key essays publishers dared not print.* Chicago: New Classics House.

Ellis, A. (1968). Is psychoanalysis harmful? *Psychiatric Opinion,* 5(1), 16–25. Reprinted: New York: Institute for Rational-Emotive Therapy.

*Ellis, A. (1969). A weekend of rational encounter. *Rational Living,* 4(2), 1–8.

*Ellis, A. (1971). *Growth through reason.* North Hollywood, CA: Wilshire Books.

*Ellis, A. (1972). *The civilized couple's guide to extramarital adventure.* New York: Wyden and Pinnacle Books.

*Ellis, A. (1972). *Conquering low frustration tolerance.* Cassette recording. New York: Institute for Rational-Emotive Therapy.

*Ellis, A. (1972). *Executive leadership: The rational-emotive approach.* New York: Institute for Rational-Emotive Therapy.

*Ellis, A. (1972). Helping people get better: Rather than merely feel better. *Rational Living,* 7(2), 2–9.

*Ellis, A. (1972). *How to master your fear of flying.* New York: Institute for Rational-Emotive Therapy.

*Ellis, A. (1972). *Psychotherapy and the value of a human being.* New York: Institute for Rational-Emotive Therapy.

*Ellis, A. (1972). Psychotherapy without tears. In A. Burton (Ed.), *Twelve therapists* (pp. 103–126). San Francisco: Jossey-Bass.

*Ellis, A. (1972). *The sensuous person.* New York: Lyle Stuart and New American Library.

*Ellis, A. (Speaker). (1972). *Solving emotional problems.* (Cassette recording). New York: Institute for Rational-Emotive Therapy.

*Ellis, A. (Speaker). (1972). *The theory and practice of rational-emotive therapy.* Videotape. New York: Institute for Rational-Emotive Therapy.

*Ellis, A. (Speaker). (1973). *A demonstration with an elementary school child.* Film and videotape. Arlington, VA: American Association for Counseling and Development.

*Ellis, A. (Speaker). (1973). *A demonstration with a woman fearful of expressing emotions.* Film and videotape. Arlington, VA: American Association for Counseling and Development.

*Ellis, A. (Speaker). (1973). *A demonstration with a young divorced woman.* Film and videotape. Arlington, VA: American Association for Counseling and Development.

*Ellis, A. (Speaker). (1973). *How to stubbornly refuse to be ashamed of anything.* Cassette recording. New York: Institute for Rational-Emotive Therapy.

*Ellis, A. (1973). *Humanistic psychotherapy: The rational-emotive approach.* New York: McGraw-Hill.

*Ellis, A. (Speaker). (1973). *Rational-emotive psychotherapy: A comprehensive approach to personality change.* Cassette recording. New York: Institute for Rational-Emotive Therapy.

*Ellis, A. (Speaker). (1973). *RET and marriage and family counseling.* Cassette recording. New York: Institute for Rational-Emotive Therapy.

*Ellis, A. (Speaker). (1973). *Twenty-one ways to stop worrying*. Cassette recording. New York: Institute for Rational-Emotive Therapy.

*Ellis, A. (Speaker). (1973). *Twenty-five ways to stop downing yourself*. Cassette recording. Philadelphia, PA: American Academy of Psychotherapists Tape Library.

*Ellis, A. (Speaker). (1974). *Cognitive behavior therapy*. Cassette recording. New York: Institute for Rational-Emotive Therapy.

*Ellis, A. (Speaker). (1974). *A demonstration with a woman fearful of expressing emotions*. Videotape. New York: Institute for Rational-Emotive Therapy.

*Ellis, A. (Speaker). (1974). *Rational living in an irrational world*. Cassette recording. New York: Institute for Rational-Emotive Therapy.

*Ellis, A. (1974). *Technique of disputing irrational beliefs (DIBS)*. New York: Institute for Rational-Emotive Therapy.

*Ellis, A. (1974). The treatment of sex and love problems in women. In V. Franks & V. Burtle (Eds.), *Women in therapy* (pp. 284–306). New York: Brunner/Mazel.

*Ellis, A. (Speaker). (1975). *Demonstration with a woman with sexual and weight problems*. Videotape. New York: Institute for Rational-Emotive Therapy.

*Ellis, A. (Speaker). (1975). *Demonstration with a family*. Videotape. New York: Institute for Rational-Emotive Therapy.

*Ellis, A. (Speaker). (1975). *Interview with a man with fear of failure in love relations*. Videotape. New York: Institute for Rational-Emotive Therapy.

*Ellis, A. (1976). The biological basis of human irrationality. *Journal of Individual Psychology, 32,* 145–168. Reprinted: New York: Institute for Rational-Emotive Therapy.

*Ellis, A. (Speaker). (1976). *Rational-emotive self-help techniques*. Cassette recording. New York: BMA Audio Tapes.

*Ellis, A. (Speaker). (1976). *Rational-emotive therapy: Clinician's guide*. Cassette recording. New York: BMA Audio Tapes.

*Ellis, A. (1976). RET abolishes most of the human ego. *Psychotherapy, 13,* 343–348. Reprinted: New York: Institute for Rational-Emotive Therapy.

*Ellis, A. (Speaker). (1976). *An RET approach to the treatment of possessiveness and jealousy*. Cassette recording. New York: Institute for Rational-Emotive Therapy.

*Ellis, A. (1976). *Sex and the liberated man*. Secaucus, NJ: Lyle Stuart.

*Ellis, A. (Speaker). (1976). *Conquering low frustration tolerance*. Cassette recording. New York: Institute for Rational-Emotive Therapy.

*Ellis, A. (Speaker). (1976). *Rational-emotive psychotherapy applied to* *groups.* Film. Washington, DC: American Association of Counseling and Development.

*Ellis, A. (Speaker). (1976). *Rational-emotive therapy with individual and groups.* Videotape. Austin, TX: Audio-Visual Resource Center, University of Texas.

*Ellis, A. (1977). *Anger—how to live with and without it.* Secaucus, NJ: Citadel Press.

*Ellis, A. (Speaker). (1977). *Dealing with sexuality and intimacy.* Cassette recording. New York: BMA Audio Cassettes.

*Ellis, A. (1977). Fun as psychotherapy. *Rational Living, 12*(1), 2–6.

*Ellis, A. (Speaker). (1977). *A garland of rational humorous songs.* (Cassette recording and songbook). New York: Institute for Rational-Emotive Therapy.

*Ellis, A. (Speaker). (1978). *Albert Ellis on rational-emotive therapy.* Cassette recording. New York: Harper & Row Audio Colloquies.

*Ellis, A. (Speaker). (1978). *How to be happy though mated.* Cassette recording. New York: Institute for Rational-Emotive Therapy.

*Ellis, A. (1978). *I'd like to stop but . . . Dealing with addictions.* Cassette recording. New York: Institute for Rational-Emotive Therapy.

*Ellis, A. (1979). Rational-emotive therapy: Research data that support the clinical and personality hypotheses of RET and other modes of cognitive-behavior therapy. In A. Ellis & J. M. Whiteley (Eds.), *Theoretical and empirical foundations of rational-emotive therapy* (pp. 101–173). Monterey, CA: Brooks/Cole.

*Ellis, A. (1979). Rejoinder: Elegant and inelegant RET. In A. Ellis & J. M. Whiteley (Eds.), *Theoretical and empirical foundations of rational-emotive therapy* (pp. 240–267). Monterey, CA: Brooks/Cole.

*Ellis, A. (1979–1980). Discomfort anxiety: A new cognitive behavioral construct. Parts I and II. *Rational Living, 14*(2), 3–8; *15*(1), 25–30.

*Ellis, A. (Speaker). (1980). *Rational-emotive psychotherapy.* Cassette recording. Washington, DC: Psychology Today Tapes.

*Ellis, A. (1980). Rational-emotive therapy and cognitive behavior therapy: Similarities and differences. *Cognitive Therapy and Research, 4,* 325–340.

*Ellis, A. (1980). The treatment of erectile dysfunction. In S. R. Leiblum & L. A. Pervin (Eds.), *Principles and practice of sex therapy* (pp. 240–258). New York: Guilford.

*Ellis, A. (Speaker). (1980). *Twenty-two ways to brighten up your love life.* Cassette recording. New York: Institute for Rational-Emotive Therapy.

*Ellis, A. (Speaker). (1981). *Intelligent person's guide to dating and mating.* Cassette recording. New York: Institute for Rational-Emotive Therapy.

*Ellis, A. (1981). The use of rational humorous songs in psychotherapy. *Voices, 16*(4), 29–36.

*Ellis, A. (Speaker). (1982). *Rational-emotive therapy: A documentary film featuring Dr. Albert Ellis.* Film. Champaign, IL: Research Press.

*Ellis, A. (1983). *The case against religiosity.* New York: Institute for Rational-Emotive Therapy.

*Ellis, A. (1983). Failures in rational-emotive therapy. In E. B. Foa & P. M. G. Emmelkamp (Eds.), *Failure in behavior therapy* (pp. 159–171). New York: Wiley.

*Ellis, A. (Speaker). (1984). *How to be happy though human.* Cassette recording. New York: Institute for Rational-Emotive Therapy.

*Ellis, A. (1984). *How to use RET to maintain and enhance your therapeutic gains.* New York: Institute for Rational-Emotive Therapy.

*Ellis, A. (1984). Rational-emotive therapy. In R. J. Corsini (Ed.), *Current Psychotherapies.* Third Edition (pp. 196–238). Itasca, IL: Peacock.

*Ellis, A. (1985). Dilemmas in giving warmth or love to clients: An interview with Windy Dryden. In W. Dryden, *Therapists' Dilemmas* (pp. 5–16). London: Harper & Row.

*Ellis, A. (1985). Expanding the ABCs of rational-emotive therapy. In M. Mahoney & A. Freeman (Eds.), *Cognition and Psychotherapy.* (pp. 313–323). New York: Plenum.

*Ellis, A. (Speaker). (1985). *A guide to personal happiness.* Cassette recording. Washington, DC: Psychology Today Tapes.

*Ellis, A. (Speaker). (1985). *How counseling and psychotherapy can help prevent a nuclear holocaust.* Cassette recording. Alexandria, VA: American Association for Counseling and Development.

*Ellis, A. (1985). *Overcoming resistance: Rational-emotive therapy with difficult clients.* New York: Springer.

*Ellis, A. (1985). Two forms of humanistic psychology: Rational-emotive therapy vs. transpersonal psychology. *Free Inquiry, 15*(4), 14–21.

*Ellis, A. (Speaker). (1985). *Workshop on rational-emotive therapy techniques.* Cassette recording. Garden Grove, CA: InfoMedix and Milton Erickson Foundation.

*Ellis, A. (1986). Anxiety about anxiety: The use of hypnosis with rational-emotive therapy. In E. T. Dowd & J. M. Healy (Eds.), *Case studies in hypnotherapy* (pp. 3–11). New York: Guilford.

*Ellis, A. (1986). Bibliography. *American Psychologist, 41,* 382–397.

*Ellis, A. (1986). Comments on Gloria. *Psychotherapy, 23,* 647–648.

*Ellis, A. (1986). Do some religious beliefs help create emotional disturbance? *Psychotherapy in Private Practice, 4*(4), 101–106.

*Ellis, A. (Speaker). (1986). *Effective self-assertion.* Cassette recording. Washington, DC: Psychology Today Tapes.

*Ellis, A. (1986). An emotional control card for inappropriate and appro priate emotions in using rational-emotive imagery. *Journal of Counseling and Development, 65,* 205–206.

*Ellis, A. (1986). Fanaticism that may lead to a nuclear holocaust: The contributions of scientific counseling and psychotherapy. *Journal of Counseling and Development, 65,* 146–151.

*Ellis, A. (Speaker). (1986). *Incorporating hypnosis in RET.* Cassette recording. Phoenix, AZ: Milton H. Erickson Foundation and InfoMedix.

*Ellis, A. (1986). Rational-emotive therapy applied for relationship therapy. *Journal of Rational-Emotive Therapy, 4*(1), 4–21.

*Ellis, A. (Speaker). (1986). *Rekindling romance.* Cassette recording. Washington, DC: Psychology Today Tapes.

*Ellis, A. (1987). Critical incidents in group therapy: Rational-emotive therapy. In J. Donigan & R. Malnati (Eds.). *Critical incidents in group therapy* (pp. 87–91, 105–109, 123–128, 141–146, 166–172, 189–192). Monterey, CA: Brooks/Cole.

*Ellis, A. (1987). The evolution of rational-emotive therapy (RET) and cognitive behavior therapy (CBT). In J. K. Zeig (Ed.), *The evolution of psychotherapy.* (pp. 107–133). New York: Brunner/Mazel.

*Ellis, A. (1987). *Four decades of experience with the media.* Cassette recording, No. 19. New York & Alexandria, VA: Audio Transcripts and American Psychological Association.

*Ellis, A. (Speaker). (1987). *How to stop worrying and start living.* Cassette recording. Washington, DC: Psychology Today Tapes.

*Ellis, A. (1987). The impossibility of achieving consistently good mental health. *American Psychologist, 42,* 364–375.

*Ellis, A. (1987). On the origin and development of rational-emotive therapy. In W. Dryden (Ed.), *Key cases in psychotherapy* (pp. 148–175). London: Croom Helm.

*Ellis, A. (Speaker). (1987). *Practical applications of rational-emotive therapy.* (3 cassette recordings). Indianapolis, IN: Access.

*Ellis, A. (1987). Rational-emotive therapy: Current appraisal and future directions. *Journal of Cognitive Psychotherapy, 1*(2), 73–86.

*Ellis, A. (1987). A sadly neglected cognitive element in depression. *Cognitive Therapy and Research, 11,* 121–146.

*Ellis, A. (1987). Self-control: The rational-emotive therapy method. *Southern Psychologist, 3*(1), 9–12.

*Ellis, A. (1987). The use of rational humorous songs in psychotherapy. In W. F. Fry, Jr., & W. A. Salameh (Eds.), *Handbook of humor and psychotherapy.* (pp. 265–286). Sarasota, FL: Professional Resource Exchange.

*Ellis, A. (1987). Testament of a humanist. *Free Inquiry, 7*(2), 21.

*Ellis, A. (Speaker). (1987). *The theory and practice or rational-emotive therapy and practical applications of rational-emotive therapy*. (4 cassette recordings). Indianapolis, IN: Access.

*Ellis, A. & Abarbanel, A. (Eds.). (1961), *Encyclopedia of sexual behavior*. 2 vols. New York: Hawthorn.

*Ellis, A., & Abrahms, E. (1978). *Brief psychotherapy in medical and health practice*. New York: Springer.

*Ellis, A., & Abrahms, E. (Speakers). (1978). *Brief psychotherapy and crisis intervention*. Cassette recording. New York: Institute for Rational-Emotive Therapy.

*Ellis, A., & Abrahms, E. (Speakers). (1978). *Dialogues on RET*. Cassette recording. New York: Psychotherapy Tape Library.

*Ellis, A., & Abrahms, E. (Speakers). (1978). *Use of rational-emotive therapy*. Cassette recording. Glendale, CA: Audio-Digest Foundation and American Psychiatric Association.

*Ellis, A., & Allen, T. (Speakers). (1973). *Rational-emotive therapy applied to groups*. Film and videotape. Arlington, VA: American Association for Counseling and Development.

*Ellis, A., & Allen, T. (Speakers). (1973). *Rational-emotive psychotherapy: Interview with Tom Allen*. Film and videotape. Arlington, VA: American Association for Counseling and Development.

*Ellis, A., & Becker, I. (1982). *A guide to personal happiness*. North Hollywood, CA: Wilshire.

*Ellis, A., & Bernard, M. E. (Eds.). (1983). *Rational-emotive approaches to the problems of childhood*. New York: Plenum.

*Ellis, A., & Bernard, M. E. (Eds.). (1985). *Clinical applications of rational-emotive therapy*. New York: Plenum.

*Ellis, A., & Dryden, W. (1987) *The practice of rational-emotive therapy*. New York: Springer.

*Ellis, A., & Goulding, M. (Speakers). (1985). Evolution of rational-emotive therapy. Cassette recording. Garden Grove, CA: InfoMedix and Milton Erikson Foundation.

*Ellis, A., & Grieger, R. (Eds.). (1977). *Handbook of rational-emotive therapy*. Vol. I. New York: Springer.

*Ellis, A., & Grieger, R. (Eds.). (1986). *Handbook of rational-emotive therapy*. Vol. II. New York: Springer.

*Ellis, A., & Harper, R. A. (1961). *A guide to successful marriage*. North Hollywood, CA: Wilshire Books.

*Ellis, A., & Harper, R. A. (1961). *A guide to rational living*. Englewood, CA: Prentice Hall.

*Ellis, A., & Harper, R. A. (Speakers). (1974). *Interview with Dr. Albert*

Ellis. Cassette recording. Salt Lake City, UT: American Academy of Psychotherapists.

*Ellis, A., & Harper, R. A. (1975). *A new guide to rational living*. North Hollywood, CA: Wilshire Books.

*Ellis, A., & Knaus, W. (1977). *Overcoming procrastination*. New York: New American Library.

*Ellis, A., Krasner, P., & Wilson, R. A. (1960). An impolite interview with Dr. Albert Ellis. *Realist*, Issue *16*, 1, 9–14; Issue *17*, 7–12. Rev. Ed.: New York: Institute for Rational-Emotive Therapy. Rev. ed., 1985.

*Ellis, A., & McInerney, J. F., DiGiuseppe, R., & Yeager, R. J. (1988). *Rational-emotive therapy with alcoholics and substance abusers*. New York: Pergamon.

*Ellis, A., Rogers, C. R., & Perls, F. (Speakers). (1963). *Three approaches to psychotherapy*. Film. Corona Del Mar: Psychological and Educational Films.

*Ellis, A., & Sagarin, E. (1965). *Nymphomania: A study of the oversexed woman*. New York: MacFadden.

*Ellis, A., Sichel, J., DiGiuseppe, R. A., & DiMattia, D. J. (in press) *Rational-emotive couples counseling*. New York: Pergamon.

*Ellis, A., & Szasz, T. (Speakers). (1980). *Is mental illness a myth?* Cassette recording. New York: Institute for Rational-Emotive Therapy.

*Ellis, A., & Wessler, R. (Speakers). (1983). *Conversations with Albert Ellis*. Two videotapes. New York: Institute for Rational-Emotive Therapy.

*Ellis, A., & Whiteley, J. M. (1979). *Theoretical and empirical foundations of rational-emotive therapy*. Monterey, CA: Brooks/Cole.

*Ellis, A., Wolfe, J. L. & Moseley, S. (1966). *How to raise an emotionally healthy, happy child*. North Hollywood, CA: Wilshire Book.

*Ellis, A., & Yaeger, R. (in press). *The enormous dangers of transpersonal psychology and psychotherapy*. Buffalo, NY: Prometheus.

*Ellis, A., Young, J., & Lockwood, G. (1987). Cognitive therapy and rational-emotive therapy: A dialogue. *Journal of Cognitive Psychotherapy*. *1*(4), 137–187.

*Engels, G., & Diekstra, R. F. W. (1986). Meta-analysis of rational-emotive therapy outcome studies. In P. Eelen & O. Fontaine (Eds.), *Behavior therapy: Beyond the conditioning framework* (pp. 121–140). Hillsdale, NJ: Lawrence Erlbaum.

Epictetus. (1890). *The collected works of Epictetus*. Boston: Little, Brown.

Epstein, S. (1984). Emotions from the perspective of cognitive self theory. In P. Shaver (Ed.), *Review of personality and social psychology* (pp. 1–59). Beverly Hills, CA: Sage Publications.

*Eschenroeder, C. (1982). How rational is rational-emotive therapy? A critical appraisal of its theoretical foundations and therapeutic methods. *Cognitive Therapy and Research, 6,* 381–392.

Fenichel, O. (1945). *Psychoanalytic theory of neurosis.* New York: Norton.

Ferenczi, S. (1952). *Further contributions to the theory and technique of psychoanalysis.* New York: Basic Books.

*Forsterling, F. (1985). Rational-emotive therapy and attribution theory: An investigation of the cognitive determinants of emotions. *British Journal of Cognitive Psychotherapy, 3*(1), 15–25.

Frank, J. (1963). *Persuasion and healing.* Baltimore, MD: Johns Hopkins.

Frankl, V. (1959). *Man's search for meaning.* New York: Pocket Books.

Franks, C. M., & Wilson, G. T. (1978). *Behavior therapy: Theory and practice.* New York: Brunner/Mazel.

Freeman, A., & Greenwood, V. (1986). *Cognitive therapy.* New York: Human Sciences Press.

Freud, S. (1937). *The ego and the mechanisms of defense.* London: Hogarth.

Freud, S. (1965). *Standard edition of the complete psychological works of Sigmund Freud.* London: Hogarth.

*Garcia, E. J. & Blythe, B. T. (1977). *Developing emotional muscle.* Georgia: University of Georgia.

Glasser, W. (1965). *Reality therapy.* New York: Harper & Row.

*Golden, W. L. (1983). Rational-emotive hypnotherapy: Principles and practice. *British Journal of Cognitive Psychotherapy, 1*(1), 47–56.

Goldfried, M. R., & Davison, G. C. (1976). *Clinical behavior therapy.* New York: Holt, Rinehart & Winston.

Goldfried, M. R., & Merbaum, M. (1973). (Eds.). Behavior change through self-control. New York: Holt, Rinehart & Winston.

*Grieger, R. (1986). *A client's guide to rational-emotive therapy.* Virginia: Grieger, R.

*Grieger, R. M. (1986) (Ed.). *Rational-emotive couples therapy.* A special issue of *Journal of Rational-Emotive Therapy.* New York: Human Sciences Press.

*Grieger, R., & Boyd, J. (1980). *Rational-emotive therapy: A skills-based approach.* New York: Van Nostrand Reinhold.

*Grieger, R., & Grieger, I. (Eds.). (1982). *Cognition and emotional disturbance.* New York: Human Sciences Press.

Guidano, V. F., & Liotti, G. (1983). *Cognitive processes and emotional disorders.* New York: Guilford.

*Haaga, D. A., & Davison, G. C. (in press). Outcome studies of rational-emotive therapy. In M. E. Bernard & R. A. DiGiuseppe, Eds., *Inside rational-emotive therapy.* Orlando, FL: Academic Press.

Haley, J. (1976). *Problem-solving therapy.* San Francisco, CA: Jossey-Bass.

Harper, R. A. (1981). Limitations of marriage and family therapy. *Rational Living, 16*(2), 3–6.

*Hauck, P. A. (1967). *The rational management of children.* New York: Libra.

*Hauck, P. A. (1972). *Reason in pastoral counseling.* Philadelphia, PA: Westminster.

*Hauck, P. A. (1973). *Overcoming depression.* Philadelphia: Westminster.

*Hauck, P. A. (1977b). *Marriage is a loving business.* Philadelphia, PA: Westminster.

*Hauck, P. A. (1981). *Overcoming jealousy and possessiveness.* Philadelphia, PA: Westminster.

*Hauck, P. A. (1984). *The three faces of love.* Philadelphia, PA: Westminster.

Heidegger, M. (1962). *Being and time.* New York: Harper & Row.

Herzberg, A. (1945). *Active psychotherapy.* New York: Grune & Stratton.

*Hoellen, B., & Ellis, A. (1986). An interview with Albert Ellis. *Psychotherapy in Private Practice, 4*(2), 81–98.

Hoffer, E. (1951). *The true believer.* New York: Harper & Row.

Hollon, S. D. (1983). *Cognitive therapy and research.* New York: Plenum.

Horney, K. (1945). *Our inner conflicts.* New York: Norton.

Horney, K. (1950). *Neurosis and human growth.* New York: Norton.

*Huber, C. H. (1985). Pure versus pragmatic RET. *Journal of Counseling and Development, 63,* 321–322.

Jacobsen, E. (1938). *You must relax.* New York: McGraw-Hill

*Jakubowski, P., & Lange, A. J. (1978). *The assertive option: Your rights & responsibilities.* Champaign, IL: Research Press.

Janet, P. (1898). *Nevroses et idées fixes.* 2 vols. Paris: Alcan.

Janis, I. L. (1983). *Short-term counseling.* New Haven, CT: Yale University Press.

Janis, I. L., & Mann, L. (1977). *Decision making.* New York: Free Press.

*Johnson, N. (1980). Must the rational-emotive therapist be like Albert Ellis? *Personnel and Guidance Journal, 59,* 49–51.

Jones, M. C. (1920a). The elimination of children's fears. *Journal of Experimental Psychology, 7,* 383–390.

Jones, M. C. (1924b). A laboratory study of fear: The case of Peter. *Journal of Genetic Psychology, 31*, 308–315.

*Jones, R. (1968). *A factored measure of Ellis' irrational belief systems with personality and maladjustment correlates.* Ph.D. Dissertation, Texas Tech. College.

*Jorm, A. P. (1987). Modifiability of a personality trait which is a risk factor for neurosis. Paper presented at World Psychiatric Association, Symposium on Epidemiology and the prevention of mental disorder. Reykjavik.

*Kassinove, H., Crisci, R., & Tiggerman, S. (1977). Developmental trends in rational thinking: Implications for rational-emotive school mental health programs. *Journal of Community Psychology, 5*, 266–274.

Kelly, G. (1955). *The psychology of personal constructs.* 2 vols. New York: Norton.

Kendall, P. C. (Ed.) (1983). *Advances in cognitive behavioral research and therapy.* Vol. 2. New York: Academic Press.

Kendall, P. C., & Braswell, L. (1984). *Cognitive behavioral therapy for impulsive children.* New York: Guilford.

Kendall, P. C., & Hollon, S. (Eds.) (1979). *Cognitive behavioral interventions: Theory, research and procedures.* New York: Academic Press.

*Knaus, W. (1974). *Rational-emotive education.* New York: Institute for Rational-Emotive Therapy.

*Knaus, W. (1983). *How to conquer your frustrations.* Englewood Cliffs, NJ: Prentice-Hall.

*Knaus, W., & Hendricks, C. (1986). *The illusion trap.* New York: World Almanac.

Korzybski, A. (1933). *Science and sanity.* San Francisco: International Society of General Semantics.

*Kranzler, G. (1974). *You can change how you feel.* Eugene, Oregon: Author.

*Lange, A. J. (1979). Cognitive-behavioral group therapy and assertion training. In D. Upper & S. M. Rose (Eds.), *Behavioral group therapy.* Champaign, IL: Research Press.

*Lange, A., & Jakubowski, P. (1976). *Responsible assertive behavior.* Champaign, IL: Research Press.

Lazarus, A. A. (1971). *Behavior therapy and beyond.* New York: McGraw-Hill.

Lazarus, A. A. (1981). *The practice of multimodal therapy.* New York: McGraw-Hill.

Lazarus, A. A. (1984). *In the mind's eye.* New York: Guilford.

Lazarus, A. A. (1985). *Marital myths.* San Luis Obispo, CA: Impact.

Lazarus, A. A., & Fay, A. (1975). *I can if I want to.* New York: Morrow

Lazarus, R. S. (1966). *Psychological stress and the coping process*. New York: McGraw-Hill.

Lazarus, R. S., & Folkman, S. (1984). *Stress, appraisal, and coping*. New York: Springer.

*Leaf, R. C., Gross, P. H., Todres, A. K., & Marcus, S. (1986). Placebo-like effects of education about rational-emotive therapy. *Psychological Reports, 58*, 351–370.

Lecky, P. (1943). *Self-consistency*. New York: Doubleday/Anchor.

*Lembo, J. M. (1974). *Help yourself*. Niles, IL: Argus.

Low, A. A. (1952). *Mental health through will training*. Boston: Christopher.

Mahoney, M. J. (1974). *Cognition and behavior modification*. Cambridge, MA: Ballinger.

Mahoney, M. J. (1976). *The scientist*. Cambridge, MA: Ballinger.

Mahoney, M. J., & Freeman, A. (Eds.). (1985). *Cognition and psychotherapy*. New York: Plenum.

*Mahrer, A. R., Nadler, W. P., Gervaize, P. A., Sterner, I., & Talitman, E. A. (in press). Good moments in rational-emotive therapy: Some unique features of this approach. *Journal of Rational-Emotive Therapy*.

Marcus, Aurelius. (1890). *Meditations*. Boston: Little, Brown.

Martin, J. (1987). *Cognitive-instructional counseling*. Canada: The Althouse Press.

Maslow, A. H. (1954). *Motivation and personality*. New York: Harper & Row.

Maultsby, M. C., Jr. (1971). *Handbook of rational self-counseling*. Lexington, KY: Rational Self-Help Books.

*Maultsby, M. C., Jr. (1975). *Help yourself to happiness: Through rational self-counseling*. New York: Institute for Rational-Emotive Therapy.

Maultsby, M. C., Jr. (1978). *A million dollars for your hangover*. Lexington, KY: Rational Self-Help Books.

*Maultsby, M. C., Jr. (1984). *Rational behavior therapy*. Englewood Cliffs, NJ: Prentice-Hall.

*Maultsby, M. C., Jr. (1986). *Coping better . . . Anytime, anywhere*. New York: Prentice-Hall.

*Maultsby, M. C., Jr., & Ellis, A. (1974). *Technique for using rational-emotive imagery*. New York: Institute for Rational-Emotive Therapy.

*McGovern, T. E., & Silverman, M. S. (1984). A review of outcome studies of rational-emotive therapy from 1977 to 1982. *Journal of Rational-Emotive Therapy, 2*(1), 7–18.

McMullin, R. (1986). *Handbook of cognitive therapy techniques*. New York: Norton.

Meichenbaum, D. (1977). *Cognitive-behavior modification*. New York: Plenum.

Meichenbaum, D., & Jaremko, M. E. (Eds.). (1983). *Stress reduction and prevention*. New York: Plenum.

*Merrifield, C. & Merrifield, R. (1979). *Call me RET-man and have ball!* New York: Institute for Rational-Emotive Therapy.

*Miller, R. C., & Berman, J. S. (1983). The efficacy of cognitive behavior therapies: A quantitative review of the research evidence. *Psychological Bulletin, 94*, 39–53.

*Miller, T. (1986). *The unfair advantage*. Skaneateles, NY: Lakeside Printing.

*Moore, R. H. (1983). Inference as "A" in RET. *British Journal of Cognitive Psychotherapy, 1*(2), 17–23.

*Morris, K. T., & Kanitz, J. M. (1975). *Rational-emotive therapy*. Boston: Houghton Mifflin.

Novaco, R. (1975). *Anger control*. Lexington, MA: Lexington.

Pavlov, I. (1927). *Conditioned reflexes*. New York: Liveright.

Perls, F. (1969). *Gestalt therapy verbatim*. Lafayette, CA: Real People Press.

*Phadke, K. M. (1982). Some innovations in RET theory and practice. *Rational Living, 17*(2), 25–30.

Popper, K. R. (1959). *The logic of scientific discovery*. New York: Harper & Bros.

Popper, K. R. (1962). *Objective knowledge*. London: Oxford.

Popper, K. R. (1963). *Conjectures and refutations*. New York: Harper & Bros.

*Powell, J. (1976). *Fully human, fully alive*. Niles, IL: Argus.

Raimy, V. (1975). *Misunderstandings of the self*. San Francisco: Jossey-Bass.

*Reardon, J., & Tosi, D. (1977). The effects of rational stage directed imagery on self concept and reduction of stress in adolescent delinquent males. *Journal of Clinical Psychology, 33*, 1084–1092.

*Reardon, J., Tosi, D., & Gwynne, P. (1977). The treatment of depression through rational stage directed hypnotherapy (RDH): A case study. *Psychotherapy, 14*, 95–103.

Reda, M. A., & Mahoney, M. J. (Eds.). (1984). *Cognitive Psychotherapies*. Cambridge, MA: Ballinger.

Reichenbach, H. (1953). *The rise of scientific philosophy*. Berkeley, CA: University of California Press.

Rimm, D., & Masters, J. C. (1974). *Behavior therapy*. New York: Academic.

Riskind, J. H., & Steer, R. (1984). Do maladaptive attitudes "cause" depression: Misconception of cognitive theory. *Archives of General Psychiatry, 41*, 1111.

Rogers, C. R. (1961). *On becoming a person*. Boston: Houghton-Mifflin.

*Rorer, L. G. (1987). Rational-emotive theory: An integrated psychological and philosophical basis. Unpublished mss., Miami University, Oxford, OH.

Rose, S. D. (1980). *Casebook in group therapy: A behavioral-cognitive approach*. Englewood Cliffs, NJ: Prentice-Hall.

Russell, B. (1950). *The conquest of happiness*. New York: New American Library.

Russell, B. (1965). *The basic writings of Bertrand Russell*. New York: Simon & Schuster.

Russianoff, P. (1981). *Why do I think I am nothing without a man?* New York: Bantam.

Salter, A. (1949). *Conditioned reflex therapy*. New York: Creative Age.

*Schwartz, R. M. (1982). Cognitive-behavior modification: A conceptual review. *Clinical Psychology Review, 2*, 267–293.

Seligman, M. E. P. (1975). *Helplessness*. San Francisco: Freeman.

*Sharkey, P. W. (1981). Something irrational about rational emotive psychology. *Psychotherapy, 18*, 150–155.

*Sharma, K. L. (1970). *A rational group therapy approach to counseling anxious underachievers*. Ph.D. Dissertation, University of Alberta.

*Shorkey, C. T., & Whiteman, V. L. (1977). Development of the rational behavior inventory. *Educational and Psychological Measurement, 37*, 527–534.

*Shostrom, E., Ellis, A., & Greenwald, H. (Speakers). (1976). *Three approaches to group therapy*. Film. Corona Del Mar, CA: Psychological and Educational Films.

*Sichel, J. & Ellis, A. (1984). *RET self-help form*. New York: Institute for Rational-Emotive Therapy.

Silverman, J. S., Silverman, J. A., & Eardley, D. A. (1984). Do maladaptive attitudes cause depression? *Archives of General Psychiatry, 41*, 28–30.

Skinner, B. F. (1971). *Beyond freedom and dignity*. New York: Knopf.

*Smith, D. (1982). Trends in counseling and psychotherapy. *American Psychologist, 37*, 802–809.

*Smith, M. L., & Glass, G. V. (1977). Meta analysis of psychotherapy outcomes studies. *American Psychologist, 32*, 752–760.

*Smith, T. W. (1982). Irrational beliefs in the cause and treatment of emotional distress: A critical review of the rational emotive model. *Clinical Psychology Review, 2*, 505–522.

*Smith, T. W. (in press). Assessment in rational-emotive therapy. In M. E. Bernard & R. A. DiGiuseppe (Eds.). *Inside rational-emotive therapy*. Orlando, FL: Academic Press.

*Smith, T. W., & Allred, K. D. (1986). Rationality revisited: A reassessment of the empirical support for the rational-emotive model. In P. C. Kendall (Ed.) *Advances in cognitive-behavioral research and therapy* (Vol. 5) (pp. 63–87). New York: Academic Press.

Spivack, G., Platt, J., & Shure, M. (1976). *The problem-solving approach to adjustment.* San Francisco, CA: Jossey-Bass.

*Sprenkle, D. H., Keeney, B. P., & Sutton, P. M. (1982). Theorists who influence clinical members of the AAMFT: A research note. *Journal of Marital and Family Therapy, 8,* 367–369.

*Stanton, H. (1977). The utilization of suggestions derived from rational-emotive therapy. *International Journal of Clinical and Experimental Hypnosis, 25,* 18–26.

*Sutton-Simon, K. (1981). Assessing belief systems: Conceptions and strategies. In S. D. Hollon & P. C. Kendall (Eds.), *Cognitive behavioral interventions: Assessment methods.* New York: Academic Press.

Tavris, C. (1983). *Anger: The misunderstood emotion.* New York: Simon and Schuster.

*Thorpe, G. L., Barnes, G. S., Hunter, J. E., & Hindes, D. (1983) Thoughts and feelings: Correlations in two clinical and two nonclinical samples. *Cognitive Therapy and Research, 7,* 565–574.

*Thorpe, G. L., Hecker, J. E., Cavallaro, L. A., & Kulberg, G. E. (in press). Insight versus rehearsal in cognitive-behaviour therapy: A crossover study with sixteen phobics. *Behavioral Psychotherapy.*

Tillich, P. (1953). *The courage to be.* New York: Oxford.

*Tosi, D. J. (1974). *Youth: Toward personal growth, a rational-emotive approach.* Columbus, OH: Merrill.

*Tosi, D., & Marzella, J. N. (1977). The treatment of guilt through rational stage directed therapy. In J. L. Wolfe & E. Brand (Eds.). *Twenty years of rational therapy* (pp. 234–240). New York: Institute for Rational-Emotive Therapy.

*Velten, E. (1986). Withdrawal from heroin and methadone with RET: Theory and practice. In W. Dryden & P. Trower (Eds.), *Rational-emotive therapy: Recent developments in theory and practice* (pp. 228–247). Bristol, England: Institute for Rational-Emotive Therapy (UK).

*Walen, S. R., & DiGiuseppe, R. A., & Wessler, R. L. (1980). *A practitioner's guide to rational-emotive therapy.* New York: Oxford Press.

*Warren, R., McLellarn, R. W., & Ellis, A. (1987). Albert Ellis' personal responses to the survey of rational-emotive therapists. *Journal of Rational-Emotive Therapy, 5*(2), 92–101.

*Waters, V. (1981). *Rational stories for children.* New York: Institute for Rational-Emotive Therapy.

Watson, J. B., & Rayner, E., (1920). Conditioned emotional reactions. *Journal of Experimental Psychology, 3,* 1–14.

Weaver, G. R. (1986). *The enrichment of life.* Buffalo, NY: Prometheus Books.

Weekes, C. (1972). *Peace from nervous tension.* New York: Hawthorne.

*Weinrach, S. G. (1980). Unconventional therapist: Albert Ellis. *Personnel and Guidance Journal, 59*, 152–160.

*Wessler, R. A., & Wessler, R. L. (1980). *The principles and practice of rational-emotive therapy.* San Francisco, CA: Jossey-Bass.

*Wessler, R. L. (1984). Alternative conceptions of rational-emotive therapy: Toward a philosophically neutral psychotherapy. In M. A. Reda & M. J. Mahoney (Eds.), *Cognitive psychotherapies: Recent developments in theory, research and practice* (pp. 65–79). Cambridge, MA: Ballinger.

Wessler, R. L. (1986). Conceptualizing cognitions in the cognitive-behavioural therapies. In W. Dryden & W. L. Golden (Eds.), *Cognitive-behavioural approaches to psychotherapy* (pp. 1–30). London: Harper & Row.

*Wessler, R. L., & Ellis, A. (1980). Supervision in rational-emotive therapy. In A. K. Hess (Ed.), *Psychotherapy supervision* (pp. 181–191). New York: Wiley.

*Wessler, R. L., & Ellis, A. (1983). Supervision in counseling: Rational-emotive therapy. *Counseling Psychologist, 11*, 43–49.

Wessler, R. L., & Hankin-Wessler, S. W. R. (1986). Cognitive appraisal therapy. In W. Dryden & W. Golden (Eds.), *Cognitive-behavioural approaches to psychotherapy* (pp. 196–223). London: Harper & Row.

Wick, E. (1983). Psychotherapy focus: Old and new. *Voices, 18*(4), 34–38.

*Wiener, D. (1988). *Albert Ellis: Passionate skeptic.* New York: Praeger.

*Wolfe, J. L. (1974). *Rational-emotive therapy and women's assertiveness training.* Cassette recording. New York: Institute for Rational-Emotive Therapy.

*Wolfe, J. L. (1974). *Rational-emotive therapy and women's problems.* Cassette recording. New York: Institute for Rational-Emotive Therapy.

*Wolfe, J. L., & Brand, E. (Eds.). (1977). *Twenty years of rational therapy.* New York: Institute for Rational-Emotive Therapy.

*Wolfe, J. L., & Fodor, I. G. (1975). A cognitive-behavioral approach to modifying assertive behavior in women. *Counseling Psychologist, 5*(4), 45–52.

Wolpe, J. (1958). *Psychotherapy by reciprocal inhibition.* Stanford, CA: Stanford University Press.

Wolpe, J. (1980). Cognitive behavior: A reply to three commentaries. *American Psychologist, 35*, 112–114.

Wolpe, J. (1982). *The practice of behavior therapy.* 3rd Ed. New York: Pergamon Press.

Wolpe, J., & Lazarus, A. A. (1966). *Behavior therapy techniques.* New York: Pergamon.

*Young, H. S. (1974). *A rational counseling primer.* New York: Institute for Rational-Emotive Therapy.

*Young, H. S. (1984). Special issue: The work of Howard S. Young. *British Journal of Cognitive Psychotherapy.* 2(2), 1–101.

Zajonc, R. B. (1980). Feeling and thinking: Preferences need no inferences. *American Psychologist, 35,* 151–175.

*Zettle, R. D., & Gayes, S. C. (1980). Conceptual and empirical status of rational-emotive therapy. In M. Hersen, R. M. Eisler, & P. M. Miller (Eds.). *Progress in behavior modification* (Vol. 9) (pp. 125–162). Orlando, FL: Academic Press.

Zilbergeld, B., & Lazarus, A. A. (1987). *Mind power.* Boston: Little, Brown.

*Zingle, H. W. (1965). *Therapy approach to counseling underachievers.* Ph.D. thesis, University of Alberta.

Appendix

Sample ERT Homework Report

SAMPLE HOMEWORK REPORT

Institute for Advanced Study in Rational Psychotherapy / 45 East 65th Street / New York, N.Y. 10021

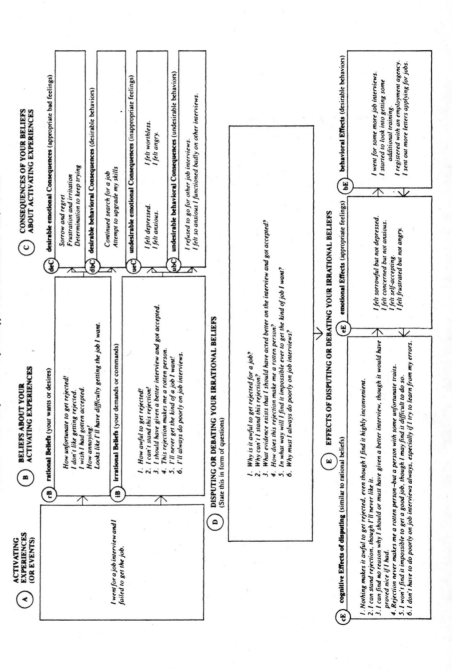

(A) ACTIVATING EXPERIENCES (OR EVENTS)

I went for a job interview and I failed to get the job.

(B) BELIEFS ABOUT YOUR ACTIVATING EXPERIENCES

(rB) rational Beliefs (your wants or desires)

How unfortunate to get rejected!
I don't like getting rejected.
I wish I had gotten accepted.
How annoying!
Looks like I'll have difficulty getting the job I want.

(iB) Irrational Beliefs (your demands or commands)

1. How awful to get rejected!
2. I can't stand this rejection!
3. I should have given a better interview and got accepted.
4. This rejection makes me a rotten person.
5. I'll never get the kind of a job I want!
6. I'll always do poorly on job interviews.

(C) CONSEQUENCES OF YOUR BELIEFS ABOUT ACTIVATING EXPERIENCES

(deC) desirable emotional Consequences (appropriate bad feelings)

Sorrow and regret
Frustration and irritation
Determination to keep trying

(dbC) desirable behavioral Consequences (desirable behaviors)

Continued search for a job
Attempt to upgrade my skills

(ueC) undesirable emotional Consequences (inappropriate feelings)

I felt depressed.   I felt worthless.
I felt anxious.   I felt angry.

(ubC) undesirable behavioral Consequences (undesirable behaviors)

I refused to go for other job interviews.
I felt so anxious I functioned badly on other interviews.

(D) DISPUTING OR DEBATING YOUR IRRATIONAL BELIEFS
(State this in form of questions)

1. Why is it awful to get rejected for a job?
2. Why can't I stand this rejection?
3. What evidence exists that I should have acted better on the interview and got accepted?
4. How does this rejection make me a rotten person?
5. In what way will I find it impossible ever to get the kind of job I want?
6. Why must I always do poorly on job interviews?

(E) EFFECTS OF DISPUTING OR DEBATING YOUR IRRATIONAL BELIEFS

(cE) cognitive Effects of disputing (similar to rational beliefs)

1. Nothing makes it awful to get rejected, even though I find it highly inconvenient.
2. I can stand rejection, though I'll never like it.
3. I can find no reason why I should or must have given a better interview, though it would have proved nice if I had.
4. Rejection never makes me a rotten person–but a person with some unfortunate traits.
5. I won't find it impossible to get a good job, though I may find it difficult to do so.
6. I don't have to do poorly on job interviews always, especially if I try to learn from my errors.

(eE) emotional Effects (appropriate feelings)

I felt sorrowful but not depressed.
I felt concerned but not anxious.
I felt self-accepting.
I felt frustrated but not angry.

(bE) behavioral Effects (desirable behaviors)

I went for some more job interviews.
I started to look into getting some additional training.
I registered with an employment agency.
I sent out more letters applying for jobs.

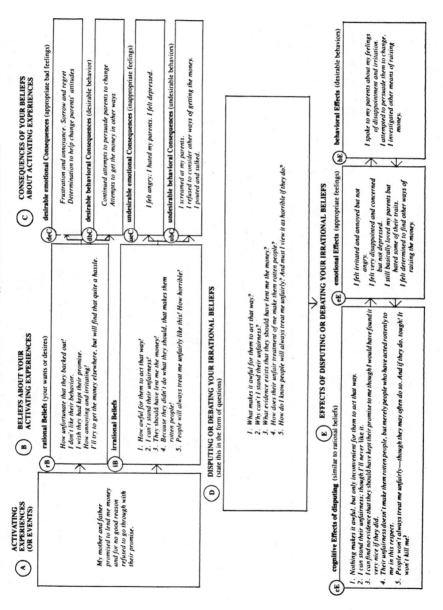

SAMPLE HOMEWORK REPORT

Institute for Advanced Study in Rational Psychotherapy / 45 East 65th Street / New York, N.Y. 10021

(A) ACTIVATING EXPERIENCES (OR EVENTS)

My mother and father promised to lend me money and for no good reason refused to go through with their promise.

(B) BELIEFS ABOUT YOUR ACTIVATING EXPERIENCES

(rB) rational Beliefs (your wants or desires)

How unfortunate that they backed out!
I don't like their behavior.
I wish they had kept their promise.
How annoying and irritating!
I'll try to get the money elsewhere, but will find that quite a hassle.

(iB) Irrational Beliefs

1. How awful for them to act that way!
2. I can't stand their unfairness!
3. They should have lent me the money!
4. Because they didn't do what they should, that makes them rotten people!
5. People will always treat me unfairly like this! How horrible!

(C) CONSEQUENCES OF YOUR BELIEFS ABOUT ACTIVATING EXPERIENCES

(deC) desirable emotional Consequences (appropriate bad feelings)

Frustration and annoyance. Sorrow and regret
Determination to help change parents' attitudes

(dbC) desirable behavioral Consequences (desirable behavior)

Continued attempts to persuade parents to change
Attempts to get the money in other ways

(ueC) undesirable emotional Consequences (inappropriate feelings)

I felt angry: I hated my parents. I felt depressed.

(ubC) undesirable behavioral Consequences (undesirable behaviors)

I screamed at my parents.
I refused to consider other ways of getting the money.
I pouted and sulked.

(D) DISPUTING OR DEBATING YOUR IRRATIONAL BELIEFS (state this in the form of questions)

1. What makes it awful for them to act that way?
2. Why can't I stand their unfairness?
3. What evidence exists that they should have lent me the money?
4. How does their unfair treatment of me make them rotten people?
5. How do I know people will always treat me unfairly? And must I view it as horrible if they do?

(E) EFFECTS OF DISPUTING OR DEBATING YOUR IRRATIONAL BELIEFS

(cE) cognitive Effects of disputing (similar to rational beliefs)

1. Nothing makes it awful, but only inconvenient for them to act that way.
2. I can stand their unfairness; though I'll never like it.
3. I can find no evidence that they should have kept their promise to me though I would have found it very nice if they did.
4. Their unfairness doesn't make them rotten people, but merely people who have acted rottenly to me in this respect.
5. People won't always treat me unfairly—though they may often do so. And if they do, tough! It won't kill me?

(eE) emotional Effects (appropriate feelings)

I felt irritated and annoyed but not angry.
I felt very disappointed and concerned but not depressed.
I still basically loved my parents but hated some of their traits.
I felt determined to find other ways of raising the money.

(bE) behavioral Effects (desirable behaviors)

I spoke to my parents about my feelings of disappointment and irritation.
I attempted to persuade them to change.
I investigated other means of raising money.

HOMEWORK REPORT

Institute for Advanced Study in Rational Psychotherapy / 45 East 65th Street / New York, N.Y. 10021

INSTRUCTIONS: Please fill out the ueC section (undesirable emotional Consequences) and the ubC section (undesirable behavioral Consequences) first.
Then fill out all the A-B-C-D-E's. PLEASE PRINT LEGIBLY. BE BRIEF!

(A) ACTIVATING EXPERIENCES (OR EVENTS)

(B) BELIEFS ABOUT YOUR ACTIVATING EXPERIENCES

(rB) rational Beliefs (your wants or desires)

(iB) Irrational Beliefs (your demands or commands)

(C) CONSEQUENCES OF YOUR BELIEFS ABOUT ACTIVATING EXPERIENCES

(deC) desirable emotional Consequences (appropriate bad feelings)

(dbC) desirable behavioral Consequences (desirable behaviors)

(ueC) undesirable emotional Consequences (inappropriate feelings)

(ubC) undesirable behavioral Consequences (undesirable behaviors)

(D) DISPUTING OR DEBATING YOUR IRRATIONAL BELIEFS
(State this in the form of questions)

(E) EFFECTS OF DISPUTING OR DEBATING YOUR IRRATIONAL BELIEFS

(cE) cognitive Effects of disputing (similar to rational beliefs)

(eE) emotional Effects (appropriate feelings)

(bE) behavioral Effects (desirable behaviors)

1. FOLLOW-UP. What new GOALS would I now like to work on? ....
....
....
....

What specific ACTIONS would I now like to take?...
....
....

2. How soon after feeling or noting your undesirable emotional CONSEQUENCES (ueC's) or your undesirable behavorial CONSEQUENCES (ubC's) of your irrational BELIEFS (iB's) did you look for these iB's and DISPUTE them?................
....
....

How vigorously did you dispute them? ....
....

If you didn't dispute them, why did you not do so?...
....

3. Specific HOMEWORK ASSIGNMENT(S) given you by your therapist, your group or yourself: ....
....
....

4. What did you actually do to carry out the assignment(s)? ....
....

5. How many times have you actually worked at your homework assignments during the past week?..........................
....

6. How many times have you actually worked at DISPUTING your irrational BELIEFS during the past week?...............
....

7. Things you would now like to discuss with your therapist or group ....
....
....

Index

211

About the Author

Albert Ellis, born in Pittsburgh and raised in New York City, holds a bachelor's degree from the City College of New York, and M.A. and Ph.D. degrees in clinical psychology from Columbia University. He has been Adjunct Professor of Psychology at Rutgers University, at United States International University, and at Pittsburgh State College and has been Distinguished Professor of Psychology at the Professional School of Psychological Studies. He served as Chief Psychologist of the New Jersey State Diagnostic Center and Chief Psychologist of the New Jersey Department of Institutions and Agencies. He has been a Consultant in Clinical Psychology to the New York City Board of Education and to the Veterans Administration. He currently holds the position of Executive Director of the Institute for Rational-Emotive Therapy. He has practiced psychotherapy, marriage and family counseling, as well as sex therapy for over forty years, and continues this practice at the Psychological Clinic of the Institute in New York City.

A Fellow of the American Psychological Association, Dr. Ellis has served as President of its Division of Consulting Psychology and as a member of its Council of Representatives. He is a Fellow (and past President) of the Society for the Scientific Study of Sex, as well as a Fellow of the American Association of Marriage and Family Therapists, the American Orthopsychiatric Association, the American Sociological Association, the American Association for Applied Anthropology, and the American Association for the Advancement of Science. The American Association of Sex Educators, Counselors, and Therapists has qualified him as a Certified Sex Educator and a Certified Sex Therapist. The American Association of Marriage and Family has appointed him an Approved Supervisor. He is a Diplomate in Clinical Psychology of the American Board of Professional Psychology, a Diplomate in Clinical Hypnosis of the American Board of Psychological Hypnosis, and a Diplomate of the American Board of Psychotherapy.

Dr. Ellis has also served as Vice-President of the American Academy of Psychotherapists, as Chairman of the Marriage Counseling Section of the National Council of Family Relations, and as an Executive Committee Member of the Divisions of Psychotherapy and of Humanistic Psychology of the American Psychological Association, and of the New York Society of Clinical Psychologists. Several professional societies have honored him: He holds the Humanist of the Year Award of the American Humanist Association, the Distinguished Practitioner Award of the Academy of Psychologists in Marital and Family Therapy, and the Distinguished Psychologist Award of the Division of Psychotherapy of the American Psychological Association. He is a Member of the National Academy of Practice in Psychology.

Dr. Ellis has served as Consulting or Associate Editor of the *Journal of Marriage and the Family*, the *International Journal of Sexology*, *Existential Psychiatry*, the *Journal of Marriage and Family Counseling* the *Journal of Contemporary Psychotherapy*, the *Journal of Individual Psychology*, the *Journal of Sex Research*, *Voices: The Art and Science of Psychotherapy*, *Cognitive Therapy and Research*, and *The Psychotherapy Patient*. He has published over five hundred papers in psychological, psychiatric, and sociological journals and anthologies. He has authored or edited forty-nine books and monographs, including *Sex Without Guilt, How to Live with a "Neurotic," The Art and Science of Love, Reason and Emotion in Psychotherapy, Executive Leadership: A Rational Approach, Humanistic Psychotherapy: The Rational-Emotive Approach, A New Guide to Rational Living, Overcoming Procrastination, A Handbook of Rational-Emotive Therapy, Brief Psychotherapy in Medical and Health Practice, A Guide to Personal Happiness,* and *Rational-Emotive Approaches to the Problems of Childhood.*